ELEGANTLY EASY LIQUEUR DESSERTS & CRÈME BRÛLÉE

ELEGANTLY EASY
LIQUEUR DESSERTS
& CRÈME BRÛLÉE

DEBBIE PUENTE

RENAISSANCE BOOKS
Los Angeles

TO MY HUSBAND, DAVID PUENTE

MY CHILDREN JOEY, STEVEN, AND COLE PUENTE

MY MOTHER, EVELYN HOWARD AND MY FATHER, SHELLY HOWARD

MY SISTERS IRIS HOWARD, JUDI JAMES, BETH LUTERAAN, AND JO ROMANSKI

MY MOTHER-IN-LAW, RALPHIE PUENTE

Copyright © 2001 by Debbie Puente

Library of Congress Control Number: 2001095765

ISBN: 1-58063-208-4

10 9 8 7 6 5 4 3 2 1

Art Direction by Lisa-Theresa Lenthall
Design by Susan Shankin
Photos by Anthony Nex
Food Styling by Alphonse
Assistance by Kirsta Marlene
Food Styling on page 63 by Christine Masterson

Published by Renaissance Books
Distributed by St. Martin's Press
Manufactured in the United States of America
First edition

ACKNOWLEDGMENTS

First and foremost, thank you to my husband, David, and my sons Joey, Steven, and Cole, for your patience, love, and understanding of the time constraints I was under while writing this book. Thank you, David, for picking up the slack at mealtimes; I think you did more cooking than I did! Every spelling-challenged author should have a child like Joey. He will be graduating from college soon with an English degree. How handy is that?! When the stress of writing really got to me, Steven and I would pack up the surfboards and sunscreen and head out to the beach. It's our very special time together. Cuddles from Cole got me through more anxiety attacks than any medicine could have. He always knew when his mommy needed a hug.

Thanks, Mom, for helping me with the grocery shopping and calling me daily to see if there was anything you could pick up for me . . . and there always was! Thanks Dad and stepmom, Barbara, for a tremendous amount of editing help and tech support in addition to love. To my mother-in-law, Ralphie, and sisters Iris, Judi, Beth, and Jo, you know how much I appreciate your support, love, and encouragement. And Judi, thanks for being my number-one proofreader!

A group of ladies deserves special mention because they were just simply always there for me while writing this book. A few for always encouraging me to make it to the gym, with rewards of going out to breakfast after, a few for providing witty catch phrases for the book, but all for the tremendous amount of fun we have together. They're my ever-loving, ever-supportive homegirls, Linda Abbott, Rani Ahmed, Debbie Berglas, Cindi Burnett, Debbie Copsey, Marla Grosslight, Jane Martins, Mary Kay McCartney, Marsha Sarowitz, Victoria Schloss, Patty Sweet, and Janet Wilder. Also thank you Vanessa Webber, Tony Silk, and Steve LeVine for friendships that have lasted over years and miles.

From the business end of my life, Heidi Rotbart, thanks for your management advice and, when I didn't always listen, thanks for not overdoing *I told you so*. I promise to become a better listener. To Leslie

Abell for your legal advice and expertise, Carrie Brillstein and Karen Appel for the PR work you put into making my crème brûlée book such a success. You are fabulous, beautiful women and I admire you both so much. To the people who made this book possible: Bill Hartley and Mike Dougherty, for believing my work worthy of publication. Abbey Park for editing. While we didn't always agree, you were always open to compromise and I really appreciated that. And especially to Lisa Lenthall, my art director and friend. Thank you for designing and directing a beautiful book. You and I worked very hard together, but we always had a great time.

To my photographer, Anthony Nex, your sense of humor (and ability to crack me up!) and kindness, not to mention your lack of ego, made the photo shoot such a joy. I absolutely loved working with you. To Alphonse, our food stylist, and his assistant, Krista Marlene, it was a pleasure to work with you both.

Thank you everyone at Sidney Frank Importing Co., with extra gratitude to Debra Porter-Licciardello, Deirdre Maher, Eileen Almanzar, Sarah Zeiler, and Pascal Courtin. Thank you everyone at Sur La Table, especially Joyce Young and Joanne Guidi. To those who offered guidance, support in one way or another, recipes, and recipe testing, I'd like to acknowledge you as well: Gloria Rosenthal, Jill Gorelick, Jer Dufresne, Joanne Pavia, Charlie Alexander, Bruce Goldish, David Feldman, Anita Potter (No. 1 Recipe Tester!), Mindy Merrell, Katy Francisco, Serge Bonnet, Michele Gioia, and Anissa Sanborn.

Much gratitude to my neighbors Steve and Stephanie Jaffe for conveniently owning a liquor store, Liquid Wine and Spirit. Also thank you Wally's Liquors, and especially Greg Forshay.

Finally, I want to thank the people who have read my books and cooked my recipes, and have written and e-mailed me expressing their appreciation. I always find it touching that you take the time to write.

A SPECIAL THANK YOU

The author and publisher would especially like to thank the management and staff of Gearys of Beverly Hills for their kind assistance as we planned the photographs that appear in this book. Gearys granted us carte blanche to the entire two floors of the store. We were encouraged to pick and choose as we wished from the almost overwhelming collection of stemware, crystal, glasses, decanters, and anything else that caught our fancy. Without question, *Elegantly Easy Liqueur Desserts and Crème Brûlée* would not appear nearly as elegant, nor would it have been as easy, without the generosity of Gearys and the unfailing assistance of customer service manager Mary Donahue.

CONTENTS

———————————

INTRODUCTION

SINCE I'M A FOOD WRITER, a cookbook author, and known to my family and friends as "ask Debbie, she's the foodie," it's only natural that when those times of year roll around when other people get computers, weekends at the spa, or the occasional BMW Roadster, I get kitchen stuff. And for some reason, which I definitely plan to ask about one of these days, over the years a lot of people have concluded that what I needed most was bottles and bottles of liqueurs.

I have received the most beautiful bottles as gifts. Tall bottles, squat bottles, earthen-ware jugs, and cut-glass decanters, all filled with liqueurs that ranged the spectrum from orange and hazelnut to spicy cinnamon, including one creamy coffee liqueur that was divided down the middle, half brown and half white. Even knowing that many of these liqueurs were quite expensive, being a partial teetotaler, my collection spent most of its time arrayed on top of the refrigerator catching the sunlight and gathering dust.

Then, when I was writing my first book, *Elegantly Easy Crème Brûlée,* I began experi-menting with different ways to flavor basic custards. Down came the bottles, off came the tops, in went a nip of this and a splash of that, and my refrigerator top has been clear ever since. Once I found what even a small amount of the right liqueur could do for a crème brûlée, I started including samplings of my exotic collection in practically every dessert I could think of.

In 1999, during one of my appearances as "The Gadget Lady" on the *Martin Short Show,* I happened to be taping a segment on making the perfect martini. Since I loved the look of the Grey Goose Vodka bottle, I chose that product to use. It wasn't long before Debra Porter-

Licciardello, the senior executive vice president for Grey Goose Vodka, contacted me. Shortly thereafter, I began one of the most rewarding phases of my culinary career—developing food recipes for Grey Goose and many of the other Sidney Frank Importing Co. products.

When people find out that I'm working on new recipes for a book about liqueur desserts, the first thing they want to know is, can an inexpensive liqueur be used instead of the brand specified in the recipe?

My answer is very simple: you don't have to cook with costly spirits to achieve good results. However, don't cook with a liqueur you wouldn't drink. The same goes for chocolate, I might add. If it isn't good enough to eat right out of the wrapper, don't use it in your desserts.

The next question almost everybody asks is, how much alcohol burns out in cooking?

A common misconception is that simmering, baking, or flaming will "burn off" the alcohol and, when ready to serve, only the flavor will remain.

A study on alcohol retention in food preparation appeared in the April 1992 issue of the *Journal of the American Dietetic Association*. Six recipes were selected to examine alcohol loss during various methods of preparation. Following are the results which represent the average of dozens of tests, on everything from pot roast in burgundy wine to flambéed Cherries Jubilee.

- Long simmering time: 5 percent alcohol remained

- Short simmering time: 35 percent alcohol remained

- Oven-baked: 45 percent alcohol remained

- Refrigerated for a short time, no heat: 74 percent alcohol remained

- Flaming: 78 percent alcohol remained

- Added to boiling sauce, off the stove: 84 percent alcohol remained

Generally, the longer something cooks, the more the alcohol will dissipate. The study also revealed that whether a dish is covered (with the cooking liquid condensing underneath the lid and dripping back in) or uncovered (with the cooking liquid evaporating) makes a difference as well. Case in point, the study's somewhat surprising findings disclosed that long refrigeration times resulted in more alcohol loss than from flaming. This is due to the fact that the refrigerated item, in this case a Brandy Alexander pie, was uncovered, allowing the alcohol to evaporate. And due to the length of refrigeration, a greater amount of evaporation took place. Since flaming is done quickly, only a small amount of alcohol burns off. Once a dish's concentration of alcohol drops below a certain level, it can no longer feed a flame. But significant alcohol can remain in the finished dish.

I know that some people might think that using liqueurs in the kitchen is an extravagance, but even a small amount can lend a delightful aromatic subtlety to a dessert while enhancing the flavors of the other ingredients. And if, unlike my friends and family, yours haven't given you a refrigerator-top full of bottles, most liquor stores have "minis" that hold just the right amount to add a touch of elegance the next time you want to make dessert something special.

POPULAR LIQUEURS AND SPIRITS

The following is not the absolute last word on everything there is to know about every liqueur ever made. I know I've left some out. But I'm a dessert cook, so it's mostly just my personal opinion of what the liqueurs that I'm familiar with taste like and what I think they go well with. So if you have a bottle of something that isn't on the following list, I hope you'll accept my apology for missing it, and understand that I couldn't sample every single one. Well, okay, I could have, but if I did, this explanation would be a lot less coherent than it is.

What Brandy Is and Isn't

As I was gathering information for this book, it soon became apparent that when it came to liqueurs, frankly, I didn't know my brandy from my eau de vie. Technically, brandy can be made from any fruit or berry. Brandy is the name for the liqueur that results from boiling the fermented juices of any crushed fruit, collecting the steam that comes off, and then letting the vapor cool so it condenses back into liquid. Boil wine made from grapes, collect the liquid that condenses, and what you have is brandy.

Now, here's the confusing part. Every cook knows the sweet, syrupy liqueur called cherry brandy. From what I've just explained, you would think that cherry brandy must be made by doing that boiling-and-cooling thing with cherries, right? Well, I thought so too. And that's when I found out about not knowing my brandy from my eau de vie.

What you get when you distill the juice from cherries, apricots, peaches, or other fruit technically is brandy, but it is not called brandy. If the brandy is made from fruit other than grapes, it is called eau de vie. And an eau de vie isn't sweet and syrupy. An eau de vie has the flavor of the fruit, but the taste is dry and slightly tart and it's clear and pours just like water.

The thick, sweet, cherry-flavored liqueur known as cherry brandy is actually grape brandy that has been infused with the flavor of cherries and sweetened with syrup. Apricot brandy and peach brandy are made the same way.

It gets even more confusing. There is another group of fruit liqueurs that are all named crème de something-or-other, such as crème de cassis, and the way they are manufactured seems to me to be the same as cherry brandy. I think I understand the eau de vie part, but why are apricot, cherry, and peach called "brandy" while other fruits are "crème"? You've got me.

Personally, I like the tart flavor of an eau de vie just as well as I like the sweeter crème or brandy. And I recommend that you try cooking with both versions too. Just keep in mind that they are not completely interchangeable. If you have your taste buds set for sweet, you should use the fruit brandy or the crème. If you want a subtle version of the same fruit flavor, try the eau de vie.

AMARETTO

A dessert chef once told me that amaretto is like marzipan in a bottle. It's made from grape brandy that has been flavored with almond extracts and crushed apricot pits, and then sweetened with syrup. I think it makes a wonderful addition to cookies, cakes, and all sorts of baked goods, whether the desserts include almonds or not.

ANIS AND ANISETTE

These two liqueurs remind me of those twisted candy-ropes that kids call black licorice. In both of these drinks, the flavor comes from macerating anise berries and anise seeds in grain alcohol. Anisette has the consistency and sweetness commonly associated with liqueurs, while anis tends to be more like an eau de vie and may be either sweet or dry.

You will find other black licorice–flavored drinks under separate headings for *Galliano* and *Pastis* which includes Pernod and ouzo, and *Sambuca.*

APRICOT BRANDY

This is one of those so-called brandies that is not a distillate of apricot and therefore not technically apricot brandy. In fact, it's made from grape brandy that has been flavored with the juice and pulp of apricots. Sometimes they grind up the apricot pits and include them in the process which, strangely enough, gives it just a hint of almond flavor.

AQUAVIT

Similar to the popular flavored vodkas, aquavit is based on distilled grain or spirits to which is added the essence of spices and fruit including anise, caraway, and orange. Although the taste of anise is clearly discernible, I find the overall flavor to be too complex to fit into the category that I call "tastes like black licorice."

BAILEYS IRISH CREAM®

This is a fairly new brand-name liqueur that was launched in 1974. Though Baileys is not the only creamed whiskey, I think it's the best-known. It's a smooth and creamy blend of fresh dairy cream, Irish whiskey, coffee, and I detect a hint of chocolate as well.

BÄRENJÄGER®

This is a brand-name liqueur based on vodka enhanced with a pleasing but not cloying honey flavor. According to German legend, beekeepers invented Bärenjäger to quiet and calm bears so they could retrieve honey from the hives in the forest.

BÉNÉDICTINE®

Originally created by Bénédictine monks in the sixteenth century, this distinctively flavored liqueur is based on cognac with a secret list of additional ingredients including juniper, myrrh, angelica, cloves, cardamom, cinnamon, vanilla, tea, and honey. The complete list of ingredients is a closely guarded secret that only three people are allowed to know. Bénédictine doesn't really taste like anything but itself. I think that its sweet and unique flavor is a nice complement when added to brandy-flavored desserts.

BRANDY

As I said in the introduction to Popular Liqueurs and Spirits, the simple explanation is that brandy is what you get when you distill grape wine. Of course, anyone who likes fine brandy just jumped out the window.

Without going into a long explanation about the soil in which the grapes are grown or the quality of the wood used to make the casks in which it's aged, brandy of varying quality is produced in most countries that have climates suitable to growing grapes.

Cognac is the most famous of brandies and is produced from grapes grown in the region surrounding the town of Cognac in the province of Charente in the western part of France.

Armagnac is France's other great brandy and comes from Gascony, a province south and east of Cognac. Armagnac is derived from a wider variety of grapes than is cognac, and the method of distillation is also different from that used in cognac.

Armagnac, cognac, and other brandies are aged in wooden casks and it is the length of aging that is considered the greatest distinguishing characteristic. The designation VS on the label of either cognac or Armagnac means it is a blend of brandies that have been aged for four to seven years, and VSOP signifies five to thirteen years. Cognac or Armanac that has aged in casks from six to forty years or longer may carry the designation Napoléon, Vielle Resérve, XO, and sometimes Hors d'Age.

There are few desserts that can't be enhanced by a touch of brandy. Although I personally don't believe there is any need to use the most expensive cognac or Armagnac in cooking or baking, I still follow the classic advice: never cook with any brandy that you wouldn't drink.

CALVADOS

What brandy is to grapes, calvados is to apples. Produced in the Normandy region of France since the 1500s, a similar drink called applejack has been made in America since the early settler days. Distilled from apple cider and aged in casks, calvados is an eau de vie that is quite dry and has the flavor of baked apples.

CHAMBORD®

A branded liqueur, Chambord is a fragrant raspberry liqueur made from framboises (raspberries) and a small amount of other fruits, herbs, and honey. Used often in glazes and sauces, it is also wonderful combined with champagne then frozen and served as a granita or sorbet.

CHARTREUSE®

Created in the early 1600s, and still made by Carthusian monks, Chartreuse is the only liqueur to have a color named after it, which is a little confusing because it actually comes in two colors: green Chartreuse and yellow Chartreuse. To further complicate things, there is a third version that is green, called Elixir Végétal, and is more closely based on the original monks' recipe. All are made from a base of grape brandy flavored with well over one hundred different herbs. The yellow Chartreuse is the most sweet and syrupy.

CHERRY BRANDY

As you already know if you read my earlier explanation about brandy, this liqueur starts with grape brandy that is then sweetened and infused with the flavor of cherries. I've known people who thought it was called Cherry Heering, but in fact Heering is simply the name of a company that manufactured a version of cherry brandy that became so well-known that people thought it was its own liqueur. Cherry brandy is sweet and perfect for preparing all kinds of desserts, toppings, glazes, sauces, and ices.

COINTREAU®

The Cointreau company has been making this complex orange-flavored liqueur since the mid-nineteenth century. It is based on a sweetened grape brandy flavored with the peel of Mediterranean oranges and green West Indian oranges. It is sweet, colorless, and very good in a wide range of baked goods.

You will also find orange-flavored alcoholic drinks listed under *Curaçao, Grand Marnier, Triple Sec,* and *Vodka L'Orange.*

THE CRÈMES

Not to be confused with creamed drinks such as Baileys Irish Cream, the crèmes contain no dairy products. These liqueurs start with a brandy base that is then sweetened and infused with the flavor of the fruit or berry that appears as part of the name. All of the crème liqueurs are perfect for glazes, sauces, granitas, or sorbets, and they add a nice touch when used to prepare a dessert that features the corresponding fruit or berry.

Crème de Banane: A perfect accent to any dessert made with bananas or other tropical fruits.

Crème de Cacao: Chocolate-flavored, it comes in white or dark. Such chocolate-flavored drinks are not only produced by distilleries but also by some of the well-known chocolate manufacturers such as Godiva and Cadbury.

Crème de Cassis: Black-currant flavored liqueur, very berry-tasting.

Crème de Fraise: Strawberry-flavored, a sweet addition to the classic shortcake.

Crème de Framboise: Anything with raspberries or chocolate is made even better by adding a splash of this sweet yet refreshing raspberry liqueur.

Crème de Menthe: Perhaps the best-known of all crèmes, it is the equivalent of liquid peppermints and comes in green or white.

CURAÇAO

From the Caribbean island of Curaçao (pronounced *koor-a-sow*), this is a liqueur that is traditionally rum-based and flavored with the dried peel of not-quite-ripe oranges. It has the wonderful aroma of island oranges, and tastes sweet with a slightly bitter undernote. Although it is colorless when manufactured, curaçao is also bottled in a variety of hues including orange, green, and, of all things, blue. Regardless of the color, all curaçaos have the distinctive orange flavor.

You will also find orange-flavored alcoholic drinks listed under *Cointreau, Grand Marnier, Triple Sec,* and *Vodka L'Orange.*

DRAMBUIE®

This famed brand-name liqueur from Scotland says on the label that it traces its history to 1745. Today it begins its life as Scotch whisky, which is then flavored with herbs and mixed with honey gathered from bees that pollinate the fragrant fields of Scottish heather.

FRANGELICO®

Created in the seventeenth century by a legendary liqueur-making hermit named Frangelico, this liqueur is brandy-based and has a nice hazelnut flavor and strong aroma.

GALLIANO®

This distinctively flavored liqueur is from Italy and is made by steeping in alcohol a secret mixture of flowers, fruits, herbs, and spices. The result is a bright yellow, sweet and syrupy liqueur that has the familiar taste of black licorice with more than just a hint of vanilla. Galliano is what you add to vodka and orange juice to make a Harvey Wallbanger, so you can imagine how well it blends into any orange-flavored dessert or topping.

GIN

A distillate of grain that has been flavored and scented by the addition of juniper berries, some gins also include small amounts of other herbs and spices depending upon the individual distiller's recipe. Although gin isn't the most obvious dessert ingredient, when you think about it, a martini sorbet or a gin fizz granita sounds pretty good. Or how about a lemon pound cake or Bundt cake with a sweetened-gin glaze?

GODIVA®

A sweet and tasty chocolate liqueur produced by Godiva Chocolatier. Three versions are now available: white chocolate, dark chocolate, and cappuccino.

GRAND MARNIER®

Louis-Alexandre Marnier took the basic concept of the curaçao-style orange liqueur, but instead of using island rum as the base, Marnier used fine cognac which, after being infused with orange, was distilled, then aged in wood. Grand Marnier is a light and sophisticated liqueur that has the richness of cognac, the flavor of Haitian oranges, and I think I detect a hint of spices as well. Fresh fruit or any orange-flavored dessert will be enhanced by the addition of this liqueur and it makes a light but distinctively flavored soufflé.

You will also find orange-flavored alcoholic drinks listed under *Curaçao, Cointreau, Triple Sec,* and *Vodka L'Orange.*

GRAPPA

Brandy is distilled from grape wine. Grappa is distilled from the skins, seeds, and other stuff that's left over from the wine process. Once known as a poor man's drink, grappa is now quite trendy and expensive, but its coarse qualities don't easily lend themselves to desserts.

JÄGERMEISTER®

This famous 70-proof German liqueur is made from a secret recipe of fifty-six herbs, fruits, and spices. Jägermeister was originally used in Germany for medicinal purposes, but in America it has found a whole new group of devotees who just like its distinctive taste. For the past two years I've been creating dessert recipes designed to take advantage of its unique flavor.

KAHLUA®

This famous brand of coffee-flavored liqueur from Mexico is, to my taste, equally as good for baking as the other well-known coffee liqueur, Tia Maria. Kahlua can be used to add a little zing to almost any dessert recipe that features coffee, chocolate, or mocha.

KIRSCH

Although kirsch is distilled from cherries, and therefore a brandy, it is not the thick, sweet, cherry brandy. Kirsch is an eau de vie and, as I mentioned in the beginning, it is refreshingly brisk or even slightly bitter to the taste. It is often used to flavor cakes, it can be added to fresh fruit, and I know one cook who swears that it gives subtle but important shading to the flavor of chocolate fondue or chocolate-brandy sauces.

MALIBU RUM®

Although there are other coconut-flavored liqueurs or spirits, Malibu is the brand name that is probably the best-known. Malibu starts with Caribbean white rum that is then infused with the flavors of coconut milk and pulp. Not overly sweet, nor syrupy, Malibu rum can enliven coconut desserts or toppings, it's an interesting complement to anything chocolate or cherry, and it's perfect with tropical-fruit desserts.

MIDORI®

I've been told that Midori means the color green in Japanese and, believe me, it is. Bright green. Really bright green. Really bright green, sweet, and flavored with what tastes to me like honeydew melon with a hint of banana. Sorbet, granita, whipped cream, fruit glazes, drizzled sauces, this is a liqueur that suggests itself in concert with anything summery or tropical.

PASTIS

The famous French brand name Pernod, and the well-known Greek drink, ouzo, both fall into the category of "tastes like black licorice" liqueurs called pastis. These drinks start with alcohol that is flavored with various combinations of herbs dominated by anise or licorice. Pernod comes out golden-colored and ouzo is clear, but they both turn cloudy when water is added to them. To my taste, Pernod is not as sweet as ouzo.

You will find other licorice-flavored drinks under separate headings for *Anis and Anisette, Aquavit, Galliano,* and *Sambuca.*

PEACH BRANDY

If you've been reading this from the top, you already know what I'm going to say. If you just skipped down here because you've got some peach brandy and you want to know what to do with it, here's the same thing I said about apricot and cherry brandy. It's not really brandy made from peaches. It's grape brandy that has been flavored with the juice and fruit of peaches. I'm just happy that it's sweet and syrupy and adds something special to peach melba and all the other delicious desserts you can make with peaches.

POIRE WILLIAM OR POIRE WILLEM

This is the pear-flavored drink that is often bottled with a real pear inside. The answer to your next question is as follows: the bottles are attached to buds on the pear trees, and the pears grow inside the bottles. When the fruit is ripe, they harvest the bottled pears and then add the liqueur.

Poire William is comparable to the fruit brandies or the crème liqueurs mentioned earlier. It is a sweetened grape spirit infused with the flavor of pear. Remember, it is not the same as the poire eau de vie, which I think might be the better known of the two. Both can be used in desserts, but the eau de vie is quite tart.

RUM

This is what you get when you distill fermented molasses, which comes from the juice of sugar cane. Rum is often aged in barrels to impart additional flavors, and it is sold as dark rum, golden or light rum, and white rum. To my mind, the flavors of the various rums taste just like their colors suggest: the darker the richer. Rum babas, buttered rum, rum cakes, rum sauces, rum and raisin, spiced rum, not to mention desserts inspired by daiquiri or piña colada—rum is a drink that dessert chefs love almost as much as brandy.

SAMBUCA

This is the well-known Italian liqueur that falls into my category "tastes like black licorice." It is in fact a grape-spirit base flavored with anise and a touch of elderberry. If you've seen people tossing back flaming shots of sambuca with coffee beans in the bottom of the glass, you know that with a little imagination there are sambuca-coffee flambé desserts just waiting to be created.

SCHNAPPS

Another variation on distilled-grain spirits to which a flavor has been imparted, the various schnapps are virtually the same as flavored vodkas. Peach schnapps is likely the best-known and is more like an eau de vie than the sweet and syrupy peach brandy.

SOUTHERN COMFORT®

Just as the brand name Drambuie is synonymous with Scotch whisky–based liqueurs, Southern Comfort has become the most recognizable name in American whiskey-based liqueurs. Owned by the same company that owns Jack Daniel Distillery, Southern Comfort combines two Southern traditions, Tennessee whiskey and Georgia peaches. The result is a sweet and distinctive peach-flavored liqueur.

STREGA

It's Italian like Galliano, it looks like Galliano, but it doesn't taste like Galliano at all. In fact it's one of those liqueurs that doesn't really taste like anything but itself. However, it has just enough citrus flavor for me to put it into my category of liqueurs that go well with orange or chocolate-orange desserts.

TEQUILA

Made from the agave plant in Tequila, Mexico, tequila is drunk mostly straight as a shot or mixed with triple sec and lime juice as a Margarita. I've been experimenting with tequila lately and you'll find one of the results on page 59, my Margarita Mousse.

TIA MARIA®

This is a rum-based liqueur flavored with extracts from Jamaican coffee beans. Similar but not identical to Kahlua, it always makes me think of Starbucks coffee with a kick. There are hundreds of desserts flavored with chocolate or coffee, and Tia Maria makes a perfect addition to practically every one of them.

TRIPLE SEC

This is both a brand name for a specific orange-flavored liqueur and the name for a category of liqueurs. I didn't mention this earlier because it's almost as confusing as the brandy or eau-de-vie thing, but the words *triple sec* are a generic term for all Caribbean Island orange-based liqueurs such as curaçao. Curaçao is itself a generic term for orange-flavored liqueurs. I think what this means is that Triple Sec is a curaçao, and curaçao is a triple sec, and Cointreau and Grand Marnier are either curaçaos or triple secs, or both. I think.

VODKA

Originally from Poland or Russia, vodka is now produced all over the world. It is an almost tasteless, superclean, rectified distillate of rye or wheat. Lately flavored vodkas have become very popular. For the past two years I've been developing dessert recipes based on Grey Goose Vodka L'Orange, and I've come to like it better than most of the other orange liqueurs.

WHISKEY OR WHISKY

Americans and the Irish spell it with an "e" and the Canadians and Scots spell it without. Except, of course, when they don't, and they spell it the other way around. It's worse than brandy and eau de vie, and I'm not going to get into it.

No matter how you spell it, this spirit is a distillate of corn, barley, wheat, rye, or oats. The grain used, the method of distillation, and the way it is aged all influence the difference in flavor between Scotch whisky, Irish whiskey, bourbon whiskey, Tennessee whiskey, and Canadian or rye whisky. Whiskey has traditionally been used to flavor all kinds of baked desserts and fruit cakes. It makes wonderful glazes and sauces (in fact I find it hard to imagine bread pudding without whiskey sauce), and for something light and summery, try a Whiskey Sour sorbet.

The makers of Jack Daniel's Tennessee Whiskey have compiled their own collection of dessert recipes, some of which they have allowed me to include in this book.

WINE

For the wine desserts in this book I've used only one medium-dry red wine, and sake, which I'm told isn't really a wine because it's made from rice not fruit. And that brings me to the reason why I wrote a cookbook about liqueurs instead of wine: If I started writing about wines, there wouldn't be any room for recipes.

Red, white, sweet, dry, domestic, imported, sparkling, fortified—the variety of wines is endless, the subtlety of flavors is complicated, and it's almost a sure bet that I'd alienate half my readers if I started telling them about wine. So I'm not taking the chance. Maybe next book.

Now, what would you like for dessert?

CAKES

Triple-Layer Piña Colada Carrot Cake
with Coconut Frosting

I combined the best elements of many different recipes to create a cake that is perfectly balanced and not too sweet. Try it—you won't be disappointed!

SERVES 10

Preheat oven to 350°F. Butter three 9-inch-diameter cake pans with 1½-inch-high sides.

In the bowl of an electric mixer, combine sugars, eggs, vanilla, and rum. Beat at medium speed until smooth. Continue beating as you add the oil. In a separate bowl, sift flour, baking soda, salt, cinnamon, ginger, and nutmeg. Gradually add the dry mixture to the wet mixture. Beat until smooth. Do not overmix. Stir in carrots, pineapple, coconut, and walnuts or pecans. Pour batter into prepared cake pans.

Bake cakes until the edges begin to pull away from the pan and a cake tester or toothpick inserted in the center comes out clean, about 45 minutes. Remove from oven and allow cake layers to cool for about 10 minutes. Turn out onto wire racks to cool completely. Frost with Coconut Frosting (see directions on following page).

¾ *cup firmly packed dark brown sugar*

1 cup granulated sugar

4 large eggs

2 teaspoons pure vanilla extract

2 tablespoons Malibu rum with coconut flavor

1 cup vegetable oil

2 cups all-purpose flour

2 teaspoons baking soda

½ *teaspoon salt*

3 teaspoons ground cinnamon

1 teaspoon ground ginger

¼ *teaspoon grated nutmeg*

3 cups grated carrots (about 1 pound)

1 8-ounce can crushed pineapple, drained

1 cup shredded or flaked coconut

1 cup chopped walnuts or pecans

Coconut Frosting

2 8-ounce packages cream
   cheese, softened

½ cup (1 stick) unsalted
   butter, at room temperature

1 teaspoon pure vanilla
   extract

2 tablespoons Malibu rum
   with coconut flavor

3 cups powdered sugar

1 8-ounce can crushed
   pineapple, drained

1 cup coconut chips
   (available at most health
   food markets)

In the bowl of an electric mixer, combine cream cheese, butter, vanilla, and rum. Beat until smooth. Slowly beat in the sugar. Stir in the pineapple. Frost the tops of two of the cake layers, then place one on top of the other. Top with the third cake layer. Frost the top of the third layer, then the sides of the entire cake. Sprinkle with coconut chips.

Chocolate Melt Cakes
with Chocolate L'Orange Sauce

---

*I have the wonderful ladies at Sur La Table in Westlake Village, California,
to thank for this decadent dessert. This is my favorite chocolate cake and I make it often.
You can use any favorite orange liqueur in the sauce, such as Grand Marnier,
Cointreau, or Grey Goose Vodka L'Orange. The batter can be made a day ahead and
kept chilled until ready to bake. The sauce can be prepared up to a week ahead.
They are slightly underbaked so the chocolate center oozes when cut.*

SERVES 6

Preheat oven to 450°F. Generously butter six 1-cup ramekins. Dust with granulated sugar, knocking out excess. Stir chocolate and butter in a medium saucepan over low heat until melted, or melt in a microwave-safe bowl on the defrost setting for about 5 minutes. Stir and keep warm. Using an electric mixer on lowest speed, mix egg whites and yolks for 1 minute. Slowly add sugar, warm chocolate mixture, and flour, incorporating each before adding the next. Do not overmix. Pour batter into ramekins. Arrange ramekins on baking sheet for easier handling when transferring to and from oven.

Bake until sides are set and cakes look puffed, but centers remain soft and liquid, about 12 minutes. (If ramekins are larger than 1 cup, increase baking time to 14 minutes.) Remove from oven and baking sheet. Allow to cool for a few minutes. Run a thin knife around cakes to loosen. Place serving plate on top of ramekin. Invert cake onto plate and remove ramekin. Repeat with remaining cakes. Spoon or drizzle L'Orange Sauce (see directions on following page) around cakes. Serve with freshly whipped cream or ice cream.

8 ounces dark or bittersweet chocolate, chopped

10 tablespoons (1¼ sticks) unsalted butter

3 large eggs, separated

1½ cups powdered sugar

½ cup cake flour

Chocolate L'Orange Sauce

1 cup heavy whipping cream

6 ounces fine-quality dark or bittersweet chocolate, finely chopped or grated (1 cup)

2 tablespoons unsalted butter

3 tablespoons Grey Goose Vodka L'Orange or other orange liqueur

In a medium saucepan, bring cream to a simmer over moderate heat; remove from heat. Add chocolate and butter, whisking until smooth. Whisk in orange liqueur.

Leftover L'Orange Sauce is my secret ingredient for the very best Chocolate Buttercream Frosting (page 38). It also makes a wonderful ice cream topping.

Jack Daniel's Chocolate-Chip Praline Celebration Cake
with Hot Buttered Whiskey Glaze

This cake looks and tastes like a giant chocolate chip cookie!

SERVES 10

Preheat oven to 325°F. Grease a 10-inch tube pan. Combine flour, baking powder, and salt; set aside.

Melt butter in a 3-quart or larger saucepan over low heat. Remove from heat. Add brown sugar, eggs, flour mixture, and whiskey, stirring well after each. Pour batter into prepared pan. Sprinkle evenly with pecans and chocolate chips.

Bake about 1 hour or until center of cake is firm and edges begin to pull away from sides of pan. Cool in pan for 10 minutes. Turn out onto wire rack and cool completely. Drizzle with Hot Buttered Whiskey Glaze (recipe below) and serve.

2¼ cups all-purpose flour

2¼ teaspoons baking powder

½ teaspoon salt

1 cup (2 sticks) unsalted butter

2 cups firmly packed dark brown sugar

4 eggs

½ cup Jack Daniel's Tennessee Whiskey

1 cup chopped pecans

1 6-ounce package chocolate chips

Hot Buttered Whiskey Glaze

Place all ingredients in a large bowl. By hand or with an electric mixer, blend until smooth.

¼ cup butter, melted

2 cups powdered sugar

3 tablespoons Jack Daniel's Tennessee Whiskey

1 teaspoon vanilla

Brandy Pound Cake Layers with Mixed Berries

Recently my son Steven celebrated a birthday. Due to moderate injuries
he received while skateboarding, he was unable to participate
in his favorite activity, snowboarding. I wanted to make his birthday special,
and since he doesn't care for desserts that are too sweet or loaded with frosting,
I created this fresh, light, and wildly delicious variation of pound cake.
It was a huge success. Steven said it was the best cake he'd ever had!

SERVES 10

4 cups mixed berries
(raspberries, blueberries,
boysenberries, blackberries,
or sliced strawberries)

¼ cup Chambord, crème de
cassis, or other dark berry
liqueur

2 cups (4 sticks) unsalted
butter, at room temperature,
plus more for greasing

2 cups sugar

12 eggs, separated

½ cup brandy

1 teaspoon pure vanilla extract

¼ teaspoon salt

1 teaspoon baking powder

3¼ cups cake flour (or 3 cups
all-purpose flour), sifted
twice

2 cups heavy whipping cream

Fresh mint sprigs for
garnish

Preheat oven to 350°F. Butter two 9-inch-diameter cake pans with 2-inch-high sides. Toss berries with berry liqueur. Set aside until ready to assemble, tossing occasionally.

Using an electric mixer, cream butter on medium speed until fluffy, about 5 minutes. While continuing to mix, add sugar, then egg yolks, one at a time. Add brandy, vanilla, and salt. In a separate bowl, combine baking powder and flour, whisking to distribute evenly. Add flour mixture one cup at a time to the wet ingredients, mixing on lowest speed until batter is just blended. Do not over mix.

In a clean bowl, whip egg whites until stiff peaks form. Fold into batter until well incorporated. Pour batter into cake pans. Smooth tops. Bake until the edges begin to pull away from the pan and a cake tester or toothpick inserted in the center comes out clean, about 40 minutes. Turn out onto wire racks to cool completely.

Place electric-mixer bowl and beaters in freezer for 10 minutes. Remove. Beat whipping cream on medium-high speed until soft peaks form, about 4 minutes. If you really like the flavor of brandy, beat in 1 tablespoon

CONTINUED

granulated sugar to stiffen the whipped cream, then beat in 1 teaspoon brandy. Sample, then gradually add sugar and brandy to taste.

Transfer first layer of cake to serving platter. Spoon liquid from fruit-and-liqueur mixture over layer, then top with half the whipped cream and half the berries. Top with second layer and repeat with remaining liquid, whipped cream, and berries. Garnish with mint sprigs.

VARIATION

Chocolate Buttercream Frosting

Prepare Brandy Pound Cake as above,
omitting berries, liqueur, and whipped cream. Frost with a chocolate buttercream frosting
for a much richer cake with a hint of Armagnac or orange.

½ *cup (1 stick) butter, at room temperature*

3 *cups powdered sugar, sifted*

½ *cup unsweetened cocoa powder, sifted*

⅓ *cup whipping cream, half-and-half, or whole milk*

1 *teaspoon vanilla extract*

½ *cup chocolate sauce, slightly warmed to pouring consistency (Chocolate Armagnac-Spiked Fondue [page 132] or Chocolate L'Orange Sauce [page 34])*

Cream butter using an electric mixer on medium-high speed until fluffy. Add powdered sugar, cocoa, and cream, beating to spreading consistency (additional milk or cream may be needed). Add vanilla and chocolate sauce and beat until smooth. Frost cake and serve.

Almond-Amaretto Cream Cake

Serve slices of this moist cake with raspberry jam for tea or brunch.
For a more sophisticated dessert, serve with Amaretto Whipped Cream (page 72).
Need a great gift idea? Bake mini loaves for your friends.

SERVES 10

Preheat oven to 350°F. Butter a standard 10-inch Bundt pan (or five 5 x 3-inch loaf pans). Dust pan with flour; tap out excess. Using an electric mixer on high speed, cream butter and almond paste until smooth. Gradually beat in sugar and eggs, one at a time.

In a small bowl, combine flour, baking powder, and salt. Reduce mixer speed to low. Gradually add flour mixture to butter mixture, alternating with amaretto and half-and-half, making sure to begin and end with flour mixture.

Sprinkle the almonds and 1 tablespoon sugar inside the pan. (When turned out, or inverted, they will be on top of the cake.) Pour the batter into the pan. Bake 45 to 55 minutes (35 to 40 minutes for the smaller cakes), or until top is a light golden brown and a cake tester or toothpick comes out clean. Cool in the pan on a wire rack for 10 minutes. Carefully cut around the edges with a sharp knife to release it from the pan; turn out onto a serving plate. Brush with additional amaretto. Cool before serving.

½ cup (1 stick) unsalted butter, at room temperature

1 7-ounce package almond paste

1⅓ cups sugar, plus an additional 1 tablespoon for sprinkling

3 large eggs

2 cups all-purpose flour

1 teaspoon baking powder

Pinch (⅛ teaspoon) salt

½ cup Amaretto, plus more for brushing finished cake

½ cup half-and-half or whole milk

½ cup sliced almonds

Aunt Pittypat's Pecan Pound Cake

*Lynne Tolley, Jack Daniel's great-grandniece and proprietress of Miss Mary Bobo's
Boarding House in Lynchburg, Tennessee, created this recipe to celebrate the fiftieth anniversary
of the film classic* Gone with the Wind. *Miss Mary Bobo's is a famous establishment
that started as a traveler's hotel in 1867. Not only is Miss Tolley the proprietress,
but she is also an official taster at Jack Daniel Distillery.
For more information about Jack Daniel's or Lynchburg, log on to www.jackdaniels.com.*

SERVES 8

1 cup (2 sticks) unsalted butter, at room temperature

2½ cups sugar

6 eggs

3 cups sifted cake flour, plus more for dusting

2 teaspoons baking powder

1 teaspoon salt

½ teaspoon nutmeg

1 cup sour cream

½ cup Jack Daniel's Tennessee Whiskey

1 cup finely chopped pecans

Preheat oven to 325°F. Grease and flour a 10-inch Bundt pan. In a large mixing bowl at medium speed, beat butter and sugar until light and fluffy. Add eggs, one at a time, beating until smooth. Sift together flour, baking powder, salt, and nutmeg. Add to sugar mixture, alternating with sour cream and whiskey, making sure to begin and end with flour. Beat until well blended. Fold in pecans.

Pour batter into prepared pan. Bake 1 hour or until a cake tester or toothpick inserted in center comes out clean. Cool in pan 15 minutes, then turn out onto a wire rack and finish cooling. Pour Gone with the Wind Glaze (recipe below) over cake and decorate with pecan halves if desired.

Gone with the Wind Glaze

2 cups powdered sugar

1 tablespoon Jack Daniel's Tennessee Whiskey

Approximately 2 teaspoons water

Mix powdered sugar, Jack Daniel's, and water to make a pourable glaze. Beat until smooth.

Glazed Honeycakes

These little cakes are a welcome addition to an afternoon tea. The low oven temperature and longer-than-usual baking time creates a shortbread-like texture.

YIELDS ABOUT 1 DOZEN

Preheat oven to 250°F. Place anise seeds, flour, cornmeal, baking powder, brown sugar, and butter in the bowl of a food processor. Process until mixture resembles coarse meal. Add egg yolk, Bärenjäger, and whipping cream. Pulse only until moist. Mixture will look crumbly but will hold its shape when pressed. Press a spoonful of the mixture into the palm of your hand. Shape into a ball, then flatten into a disk about 1 inch thick. Repeat until you have about 12 disks.

Place disks on baking sheet and bake 45 minutes or until cakes are pale golden. Remove from oven and cool slightly.

- *1½ teaspoons anise seeds*
- *1¼ cups all-purpose flour*
- *⅓ cup yellow cornmeal*
- *1 teaspoon baking powder*
- *¼ cup firmly packed golden or light brown sugar*
- *1 stick (½ cup) unsalted butter, cut into pieces and chilled*
- *1 egg yolk*
- *1 tablespoon Bärenjäger honey liqueur*
- *¼ cup heavy whipping cream*

Bärenjäger Glaze

In a bowl, blend Bärenjäger and powdered sugar until smooth. Add cream if desired. Drizzle glaze over cooled cakes.

- *2 tablespoons Bärenjäger honey liqueur*
- *¾ cup powdered sugar*
- *1 to 2 tablespoons cream (optional)*

Rum Baba
with Rum-Apricot Syrup

A baba is a yeast cake soaked in rum syrup.

This is a simple recipe, the perfect ending to a weekend brunch.

SERVES 6

1 envelope (2 teaspoons) active dry yeast

1 tablespoon sugar

¼ cup lukewarm milk

¾ cup all-purpose flour, divided

1 large egg

¼ teaspoon salt

3 tablespoons unsalted butter, cut into pieces and softened, plus more for greasing

Preheat oven to 375°F. Butter six baba molds, 6-ounce ramekins, or muffin tins. In the bowl of an electric mixer, with the mixer turned off, proof yeast with sugar and milk for 5 minutes or until the mixture is foamy and puffy. Add ¼ cup flour, stirring until smooth. Cover bowl with a tea towel or plastic wrap and allow to rise in a warm place for 30 minutes or until mixture doubles. (You may also let the dough rise in a gas oven with just the heat from the pilot light. If your kitchen is very cold, however, turn on the oven for a minute or two, then turn it off and place the dough inside.)

In a small bowl, whisk together egg and salt. To the yeast mixture, add the remaining ½ cup flour in two batches, alternating with the egg mixture. Beat well at low speed after each addition. Add the butter, one piece at a time, beating well after each addition. (The dough will be soft and sticky.) Divide the dough among the molds, ramekins, or tins. Allow the babas to rise in a warm place until puffy, 30 to 40 minutes.

Bake babas 15 minutes or until golden. While babas are baking, prepare Rum-Apricot Syrup (see directions on page 44).

Rum-Apricot Syrup

¼ cup apricot jam

½ cup dark rum

1 tablespoon sugar

In a small saucepan, combine jam, rum, and sugar. Bring to a boil over high heat. Reduce heat and simmer, stirring frequently, for about 10 minutes or until thick and glossy. (If glaze becomes too thick, add an additional teaspoon of rum.)

When babas are done, remove from oven and turn out onto a cooling rack set over a baking tray. Using a toothpick, poke holes all over. Brush babas with the warm glaze until well soaked. (Excess glaze can be reserved for drizzling over serving plate.) Serve warm or at room temperature.

CRÈME

BRÛLÉES

MY 1998 BOOK *Elegantly Easy Crème Brûlée and Other Custard Desserts* offers everything one needs to know to make the perfect crème brûlée. Since then, I've developed many wonderful new crème brûlée recipes, and my friends have shared their special recipes with me as well.

Crème brûlée and after-dinner drinks have long been enjoyed as the finishing touch to a leisurely repast. Both are lingered over, savored, and consumed slowly, so it makes perfect sense to combine them.

To develop your caramelizing skills, I always advise that you begin with a small amount of sugar. For best results, use the Cheflamme hand-held butane torch. It offers the best control and produces a glassy crust. Melt the sugar until you have reached the desired thickness. If you don't have a torch, your oven broiler will work fine.

Be extremely cautious when using a torch to caramelize custards containing alcohol. The burning alcohol could cause the caramelizing sugar to splatter. The custards should be at least 5 inches away from the heat source. If necessary, an inverted roasting pan can be used to elevate the custards and position them closer to the heat. Place custards on a baking sheet or jelly roll pan for easier handling. The sugar will melt in as little as 2 minutes, so watch carefully. (If using the broiler method to caramelize, it's best to place chilled custards in a pan filled with ice before caramelizing the tops. This will ensure cold, firm custards.)

Bärenjäger Crème Brûlée

In January 2001, I had the honor of preparing dessert for my hero, Julia Child. She was in town for a book signing at the local Sur La Table gourmet cooking store, and crème brûlée was the dessert of choice for the private luncheon held in her honor. Since crème brûlée is my specialty, I was asked to prepare and serve my Bärenjäger Crème Brûlée at the luncheon. Not only did Julia eat every bite, she proclaimed it to be "Perfect!" Julia, I'm your biggest fan!

SERVES 4 (LARGE SERVINGS)

Preheat oven to 300°F. In a large bowl, whisk together egg yolks and sugar until sugar has dissolved and mixture is thick and pale yellow. Add cream, vanilla, and Bärenjäger and continue to whisk until well blended. Strain into a large bowl, skimming off any foam or bubbles.

Divide mixture among four 8-ounce individual soufflé dishes or ramekins. Place the custards in a deep pan. Fill pan with warm water until it reaches halfway up the sides of the cups. Bake until set around the edges, about 50 minutes. The centers should jiggle slightly like gelatin when tapped, but should not be liquidy. Remove cups from water bath. Allow to cool. Cover with plastic wrap and chill in refrigerator, for at least 2 hours, or up to 2 days in advance.

When ready to serve, sprinkle about 2 teaspoons sugar over each custard. Follow the instructions for caramelizing the sugar on page 46. Re-chill custards for a few minutes before serving.

8 egg yolks

⅓ cup granulated sugar

2 cups heavy whipping cream

1 teaspoon pure vanilla extract

¼ cup Bärenjäger honey liqueur

Approximately 3 tablespoons granulated sugar for caramelizing

Crème Brûlée L'Orange with Rose Petals

2 teaspoons pure vanilla
extract

2 tablespoons Grey Goose
Vodka L'Orange

Approximately 3
tablespoons granulated
sugar for caramelizing

Rose petals

Prepare as on page 47 with the following modifications: use 2 teaspoons pure vanilla extract and substitute 2 tablespoons Grey Goose Vodka L'Orange for the Bärenjäger. Scatter rose petals over dish before serving.

Chocolate Raspberry Crème Brûlée

The raspberries, cream, and chocolate make a great combination in this appealing dessert.

SERVES 6

Preheat oven to 300°F. In a medium saucepan, place cream, half-and-half, and sugar. Over medium heat, bring to simmer and add chocolate, stirring or whisking until smooth. Remove from heat and set aside.

Place Chambord in a small saucepan. Simmer over medium heat until reduced by half, about 10 minutes. Whisk Chambord into chocolate mixture.

On medium-high speed, beat egg yolks and eggs until pale yellow, about 4 minutes. Beat in chocolate mixture. Add vanilla and mix until all ingredients are well incorporated.

Divide mixture among six 1-cup ramekins or custard cups. Place the custard cups in a deep pan. Fill pan with warm water until it reaches halfway up the sides of the cups. Bake until set around edges, about 50 minutes. The centers should jiggle slightly like gelatin when tapped, but should not be liquidy. Remove cups from water bath. Allow to cool. Cover with plastic wrap and chill in refrigerator for at least 2 hours or up to 2 days in advance.

When ready to serve, sprinkle about 2 teaspoons sugar over each custard. Follow instructions for caramelizing on page 46.

Garnish with raspberries. If desired, sprinkle a small amount of sugar over berries and lightly caramelize.

1 cup heavy whipping cream

1 cup half-and-half

⅓ cup sugar

6 ounces bittersweet chocolate, chopped

½ cup Chambord or raspberry liqueur

6 large egg yolks

2 large eggs

1 teaspoon pure vanilla extract

Approximately 3 tablespoons granulated sugar for caramelizing

Raspberries for garnish

Calvados Crème Brûlée with Apple Compote

Lane Crowther, cookbook author and contributing editor for Bon Appetit *magazine, created this recipe exclusively for Cooking.com, my favorite Internet cookware site.*

SERVES 6

1½ tablespoons unsalted butter

2 Red Delicious apples (about 12 ounces), peeled, cored, and cut into ½-inch slices (about 1½ cups)

¼ cup pure maple syrup

½ teaspoon pumpkin pie spice

3 tablespoons Calvados or apple brandy, divided

2½ cups heavy whipping cream

¼ cup packed golden or light brown sugar

½ vanilla bean, split lengthwise

7 large egg yolks

Approximately 3 tablespoons granulated sugar for caramelizing

Preheat oven to 325°F. Heat a large skillet over medium heat. Add butter and cook until golden brown, about 2 minutes. Add apples, syrup, and spice. Sauté until juices evaporate and apples caramelize, about 8 minutes. Remove from heat. Add 1 tablespoon Calvados. Divide apple slices evenly among six 6-ounce individual soufflé dishes or ramekins.

Place cream and brown sugar in a medium saucepan. Scrape out seeds from vanilla bean and add seeds and bean to saucepan. Bring to simmer, stirring to dissolve sugar. Stir in remaining 2 tablespoons Calvados. Remove from heat. Remove bean.

Beat egg yolks in a large bowl. Gradually whisk in hot cream mixture. Using a ladle, divide custard evenly over apple slices without dislodging apples from bottom of cup.

Place custard cups in a deep pan. Fill pan with warm water until it reaches halfway up the sides of the cups. Bake until set around the edges, about 25 minutes. The centers should jiggle slightly like gelatin when tapped, but should not be liquidy. Allow to cool. Cover with plastic wrap and chill in refrigerator for at least 2 hours or up to 2 days in advance.

When ready to serve, sprinkle about 2 teaspoons sugar over each custard. Follow the instructions for caramelizing the sugar on page 46. Re-chill custards for a few minutes before serving.

Mocha Crème Brûlée

Smooth, rich, and creamy, this crème brûlée
is spectacular for so many reasons.
For the liqueur, I prefer using Godiva's white, dark, or cappuccino flavors.
If you're a fan of chocolate mint, try Vandermint.

SERVES 4

2 cups heavy whipping cream

2 teaspoons instant espresso powder

4 egg yolks

¼ cup granulated sugar

½ cup chocolate liqueur

1 teaspoon pure vanilla extract

Approximately 3 tablespoons granulated sugar for caramelizing

Preheat oven to 300°F .In a medium saucepan over medium heat, heat cream and espresso powder until hot but not boiling. Stir until espresso is dissolved. Remove from heat and set aside.

Beat or whisk egg yolks with sugar until pale yellow, about 4 minutes. Whisk in hot cream, chocolate liqueur, and vanilla. Whisk until all ingredients are well incorporated.

Divide mixture among four 6-ounce ramekins or custard cups. Place the custard cups in a deep pan. Fill pan with warm water until it reaches halfway up the sides of the cups. Bake until set around the edges, about 50 minutes. The centers should jiggle slightly like gelatin when tapped, but should not be liquidy. Remove cups from water bath. Allow to cool. Cover with plastic wrap and chill in refrigerator for at least 2 hours or up to 2 days in advance.

When ready to serve, sprinkle about 2 teaspoons sugar over each custard and follow the instructions for caramelizing the sugar on page 46.

Classic Crème Brûlée
and Variations

The following recipes first appeared in Elegantly Easy Crème Brûlée and Other Custard Desserts. *They're so good, I just had to include them here. For each of these variations, begin with the recipe for Classic Crème Brûlée below. The amounts given yield a mild, light flavor. Adjust amounts to your liking.*

SERVES 4 (LARGE SERVINGS)

Preheat oven to 300°F. In a large bowl, whisk together egg yolks and sugar until sugar has dissolved and mixture is thick and pale yellow. Add cream and vanilla. Continue to whisk until well blended. Strain into a large bowl, skimming off any foam or bubbles.

Divide mixture among four 8-ounce individual soufflé dishes or ramekins. Place the custards in a deep pan. Fill pan with warm water until it reaches halfway up the sides of the cups. Bake until set around the edges, about 50 minutes. The centers should jiggle slightly like gelatin when tapped, but should not be liquidy. Remove cups from water bath. Allow to cool. Cover with plastic wrap and chill in refrigerator for at least 2 hours or up to 2 days in advance.

When ready to serve, sprinkle about 2 teaspoons sugar over each custard. Follow the instructions for caramelizing the sugar on page 46. Re-chill custards for a few minutes before serving.

8 egg yolks

⅓ cup granulated white sugar

2 cups heavy whipping cream

1 teaspoon pure vanilla extract

Approximately 3 tablespoons granulated sugar for caramelizing

For the following variations (see pages 54–56), add the indicated ingredient(s) after adding the cream and vanilla but before straining.

Amaretto Crème Brûlée

---

3 *tablespoons Amaretto*

⅛ *teaspoon almond extract*

Mix in Amaretto plus almond extract.

Irish Coffee Crème Brûlée

---

1 *tablespoon Irish whiskey*

1 *heaping tablespoon (about 4 teaspoons) instant coffee*

Mix in Irish whiskey plus instant coffee.

Frangelico Crème Brûlée

---

2 *tablespoons Frangelico*

1 *heaping tablespoon (about 4 teaspoons) instant coffee (optional)*

Mix in Frangelico. Option: Add instant coffee.

Kahlua Crème Brûlée

Mix in Kahlua plus instant espresso powder.

¼ cup Kahlua

¼ tablespoon instant espresso powder

Margarita Crème Brûlée

Mix in tequila, orange liqueur (such as Grand Marnier or Triple Sec), and lime juice.

3 tablespoons tequila

2 tablespoons orange liqueur

2 tablespoons lime juice

White Russian Crème Brûlée

Mix in vodka and Kahlua.

2 tablespoons vodka

2 tablespoons Kahlua

Cassis Crème Brûlée

---

2 tablespoons cassis

½ cup black currant preserves

Mix in cassis plus black currant preserves.

Bourbon Crème Brûlée

¼ cup bourbon whiskey

Mix in good-quality bourbon whiskey.

Irish Cream Crème Brûlée

---

3 tablespoons Irish Cream

Mix in good-quality Irish Cream, such as Baileys or Emmet's.

Cognac Crème Brûlée

¼ cup Cognac

Mix in Cognac.

Mississippi Mud Crème Brûlée

---

2 tablespoons Southern Comfort

2 tablespoons coffee liqueur

Mix in Southern Comfort and coffee liqueur.

MOUSSES

SOUFFLÉS

and

PUDDINGS

Margarita Mousse

This mousse tastes just like a margarita cocktail—it's delicious. I like to serve it in margarita glasses with a lime wheel for garnish. For an authentic look, moisten the rim of each glass with a lime wedge and dip in sugar before filling with mousse.

SERVES 8

In a small bowl, combine ¼ cup water with gelatin and stir. Set aside to soften for about 5 minutes. In the bowl of an electric mixer, beat egg yolks until pale, about 5 minutes. Set aside.

In a medium saucepan, combine ½ cup sugar, ¼ cup water, and ¼ cup lime juice. Bring to a boil. Cook until sugar dissolves, about 3 minutes. Remove from heat and stir in the softened gelatin until the gelatin dissolves. Stir in the tequila, Triple Sec, and remaining ½ cup lime juice.

Slowly pour the hot sugar mixture into the egg yolks, beating until smooth. Using a rubber spatula, occasionally scrape the bottom and sides of the bowl. Place the bowl inside a larger bowl filled with ice.

In a chilled bowl, beat cream on high speed until soft peaks form. Cover and refrigerate. In a separate bowl, beat egg whites on high speed until soft peaks form. While beating, sprinkle in the remaining ½ cup sugar and beat until the whites form stiff, glossy peaks.

Stir about one-third of the beaten egg whites into the egg yolk mixture until incorporated. Fold in the remaining egg whites and all of the whipped cream, incorporating well. Cover tightly and refrigerate for at least 2 hours.

Spoon or pipe mousse into glasses and garnish as mentioned above.

½ cup water, divided

1 envelope (1 tablespoon) unflavored gelatin

6 eggs, separated

1 cup sugar, divided

¾ cup freshly squeezed lime juice, divided

½ cup tequila

⅓ cup Triple Sec

1 cup heavy whipping cream

Lime wheel for garnish

Chocolate Cherry Mousse

This mousse is irresistible.

I often serve it over fresh sliced bananas.

SERVES 6

6 ounces bittersweet
or semisweet chocolate,
broken into ½-ounce pieces

⅓ cup cherry liqueur

2 cups heavy whipping cream

3 egg whites

2 tablespoons sugar

Whole cherries with stems
for garnish (optional)

Melt chocolate in a double boiler over simmering water, stirring until smooth. (Or, if you prefer, melt in a microwave-safe bowl on the defrost setting for about 5 minutes.) Remove from heat and add cherry liqueur, stirring until smooth. Keep at room temperature until needed.

Place cream in chilled bowl of an electric mixer. Whisk on high speed until soft peaks form. Set aside. Clean and dry bowl. In bowl, beat egg whites on high speed until soft peaks form. Add sugar and continue beating until stiff peaks form.

Add a quarter of the whipped cream to the chocolate mixture and whisk until well blended; add to egg whites. Add remaining whipped cream. Fold together gently but thoroughly.

Spoon mousse into stemmed glasses and refrigerate until set, about 1 hour. Just before serving, garnish with fresh cherries if desired.

Melon Breeze Mousse with Fresh Fruit

*This is an airy and refreshing fruit dessert
inspired by the classic melon breeze cocktail.*

SERVES 6

Combine sugar, Midori, egg yolks, and whole eggs in the top of a double boiler set over simmering water. Whisk until mixture thickens and thermometer inserted into mixture registers 160°F, about 8 minutes. Transfer to a large bowl. Stir in vodka. Place bowl in an ice bath or in the refrigerator to chill, whisking occasionally.

Using a chilled bowl and beaters, beat cream on high speed until firm peaks form. On lowest speed, add about ⅓ of whipped cream into Midori-egg mixture to lighten. Turn off mixer and fold in remaining whipped cream until well incorporated.

Divide cubed melon, pineapple, or banana chunks among decorative serving glasses or dishes. Put mousse in large pastry bag fitted with a star tip and pipe mousse around melon cubes. Cover and refrigerate. Can be prepared one day ahead.

Top each with a Maraschino cherry and serve.

1 cup sugar

½ cup Midori melon liqueur

6 large egg yolks

2 large eggs

2 tablespoons Grey Goose vodka

1½ cups heavy whipping cream

3 small ripe honeydew melons, halved, seeded, and cut into ¾-inch chunks

2 cups pineapple chunks or bananas, or a combination of both

6 Maraschino cherries

Bärenjäger Soufflé

I want to thank Pascal Courtin, personal chef to
Mr. and Mrs. Sidney Frank of
the Sidney Frank Importing Co. for this wonderful recipe.

SERVES 6

4 *tablespoons butter*

4 *tablespoons all-purpose*
flour

1 *cup whole milk*

4 *tablespoons orange*
marmalade

6 *egg yolks*

6 *tablespoons Bärenjäger*
honey liqueur

8 *egg whites*

¼ *teaspoon cream of tartar*

2 *tablespoons sugar*

Preheat oven to 350°F. Lightly butter a 2-quart soufflé dish and dust it with sugar, rotating so the sugar adheres to the butter evenly. Set aside.

Melt four tablespoons butter in a small saucepan over low heat. Whisk in flour and continue whisking until mixture comes to a simmer, about 3 minutes. Add milk; cook and stir until thick and creamy. Remove from heat. Transfer mixture to a bowl and set bowl in an ice-water bath. When cooled, add orange marmalade and egg yolks, one at a time, whisking constantly. Whisk in Bärenjäger. Set aside.

Beat egg whites on low speed for 1 minute. Add cream of tartar and increase speed to medium. When soft peaks form, add sugar gradually and continue beating until peaks are stiff but not dry. With a large rubber spatula, fold half the egg whites gradually into the yolk mixture until well incorporated. Fold in remaining egg whites gently but thoroughly. Transfer to prepared soufflé dish, filling just to the rim.

Bake soufflé until puffed and golden, about 30 minutes. Serve immediately. Be sure to use a fork to cut and serve the soufflé; a spoon will deflate it faster.

Frozen Sex-on-the-Beach Soufflé

*This chilled soufflé can be prepared up to a week in advance,
making it an ideal dessert for a busy hostess.*

SERVES 10

2½ cups raspberries,
reserving 8 to 10 whole
raspberries for garnish

2 tablespoons Chambord
or other raspberry liqueur

2 tablespoons pineapple juice

2 tablespoons Grey Goose
Vodka L'Orange

1 tablespoon Midori melon
liqueur

1 cup sugar

¼ cup water

4 large egg whites,
at room temperature

2 cups well-chilled heavy
whipping cream, divided

Fresh mint sprigs for
garnish

Cut one 30 x 11-inch strip of aluminum foil. Fold strip in half lengthwise. Wrap tightly around a 4-cup (1-quart) soufflé dish, forming a collar that extends from base of dish to above the rim. Secure ends of foil with paper clips or a short piece of cellophane tape. This will create the typical appearance of a soufflé that has risen over the top of the dish.

Puree the raspberries in a food processor. Press pureed raspberries through a fine-mesh strainer to remove the seeds. Measure out puree (should yield approximately 1¼ cups). Stir in Chambord, pineapple juice, vodka, and Midori; set aside.

Place sugar and water in a medium saucepan over medium heat. Stir until sugar is dissolved. Bring syrup to a boil. Boil without stirring until syrup reaches the soft-ball stage, 234° to 240°F, or until a drop of syrup placed in ice water holds its shape but is soft when pressed.

Beat egg whites with an electric mixer on medium speed until soft peaks form. With the mixer running, add the hot syrup in a thin stream until meringue is thick and glossy. Using a chilled bowl and beaters, whip 1½ cups cream on medium-high speed until soft peaks form, about 2 minutes. Using a metal spoon, gently fold the meringue into the raspberry puree mixture until well incorporated. Fold in the cream. Mix only until well combined. Spoon the mixture into the prepared dish, filling to the top of the foil collar. Smooth the top. Freeze for a minimum of 6 hours.

Remove from freezer 30 minutes before serving. Whip the remaining ½ cup cream. Run a small knife between soufflé and foil. Peel off foil. Using a small metal spatula or knife, smooth exposed sides of soufflé. Spoon dollops of whipped cream atop dessert, or transfer whipped cream to pastry bag fitted with a large star tip and pipe over soufflé. Garnish with whole raspberries and mint.

WHY IS IT CALLED
FROZEN SEX-ON-THE-BEACH SOUFFLÉ?

Because Sex on the Beach is the name of the popular cocktail I based my recipe on. The classic version of the drink is served in a highball glass, to which you add ice, ¾ ounce Midori, ¾ ounce Chambord, ¾ ounce vodka, then fill with pineapple juice.

Rum Raisin Bread Pudding
with Caramel Rum Raisin Sauce

Turn an ordinary bread pudding into an extraordinary dessert
by using specialty breads from the fresh bakery section of the market, then
serving it with a complimentary sauce. For this dessert, I've combined
chunky cinnamon raisin bread with a rum raisin sauce.
The sauce can be prepared up to a week in advance and warmed just before serving.

SERVES 6

1 16-ounce loaf chunky cinnamon raisin bread, cut into thick slices

6 large eggs

2 cups half-and-half

2 tablespoons dark rum

Preheat oven to 350°F. Butter a 9 x 13-inch baking dish. Layer bread slices in dish.

In a large mixing bowl, whisk together eggs, half-and-half, and rum. Pour mixture over the bread, pushing down the bread with the back of a spoon to allow the bread to absorb as much liquid as possible.

Set baking dish inside a larger, shallow pan or a second, larger, baking dish. Pour hot tap water into the outer pan until it reaches halfway up the sides of the inner pan. Bake until custard is set, about 45 minutes. Carefully remove pan from oven. Serve warm with Caramel Rum Raisin Sauce (see directions on opposite page).

Caramel Rum Raisin Sauce

In a small saucepan, warm rum and raisins. Remove from heat and let soak for about 20 minutes.

In a heavy saucepan, combine sugar and water. Stir over medium heat until sugar is dissolved, brushing down sides of pan with a wet pastry brush if sugar crystals develop. Increase heat; boil without stirring, continuing to brush down any crystals until syrup turns amber, about 10 minutes. Remove from heat. Slowly and carefully add a little of the cream to stop the cooking. Add the remaining cream. Stir in rum and raisins. Sauce will be very hot! Allow to cool and thicken, at least 5 minutes, before serving.

¼ cup dark rum

½ cup raisins

1½ cup sugar

¼ cup water

⅓ cup heavy whipping cream, warmed

CARAMELIZING TIP

Covering the saucepan with a tight-fitting lid will allow steam to dissolve any sugar crystals. However, I recommend this only for a more experienced cook who works with caramel often. Once the caramel turns amber, you must remove it from the heat immediately. Caramel turns from amber to burned in less than 1 minute.

Blackberry Pudding

For a less sweet pudding, use white or sourdough bread instead of pound cake.
You can also substitute the Framboise Royale with crème de cassis,
blackberry brandy, or Chambord. Classic Crème Fraîche (page 136)
or sour cream adds the finishing touch to this flavorful dessert.

SERVES 8

1 12-ounce loaf pound cake,
cut into thin slices
(I like Sara Lee)

2 pounds fresh or frozen
blackberries

½ cup sugar (adjust according
to sweetness of berries)

3 tablespoons fresh lemon
juice

¼ cup Framboise Royale

Classic Crème Fraîche
or sour cream (optional)

Fresh mint sprigs for
garnish

Line a medium-sized bowl (about 5-cup capacity) with cake slices, reserving slices to top the pudding. Slightly overlap or press together slices to cover any gaps.

Combine blackberries, sugar, and lemon juice in saucepan. Bring mixture to a boil, stirring gently. Reduce heat and simmer until sugar is dissolved. Taste and adjust sugar if necessary.

Sprinkle cake with Framboise. Spoon hot berry mixture into cake-lined bowl. Top with reserved slices, leaving no gaps. (The berries should be completely sealed within the cake slices.)

Cover pudding with plastic wrap and top with a saucer or plate that will fit inside the top of the bowl. Place a 1- or 2-pound weight on top and refrigerate pudding for at least 8 hours.

To serve, run a thin knife around edge of bowl to loosen pudding. Invert pudding onto a serving plate. Top with Classic Crème Fraîche (see page 136) or sour cream if desired.

Old-fashioned Butterscotch-Rum Pudding

You can easily transform this dessert into a pie or tart by pouring the pudding,
while warm, into a prepared pie crust or tart shell.

4 tablespoons (½ stick)
unsalted butter

1¼ cups packed dark brown
sugar

1¾ cups whole milk

1 cup heavy whipping cream

⅓ cup cornstarch

½ teaspoon salt

4 egg yolks

2 teaspoons vanilla

2 tablespoons Scotch whisky

1 tablespoon rum

In a medium saucepan, cook butter and brown sugar over medium-low heat, stirring until mixture is dissolved, about 2 minutes. Whisk in milk. Cook until steam rises from surface, about 5 minutes.

In a large bowl, whisk cream, cornstarch, and salt until smooth. Add to milk mixture. Cook over medium heat until thick, stirring often, about 7 minutes.

Whisk egg yolks in a medium bowl. Gradually stir in about 1 cup of the hot cream mixture. Pour into a separate saucepan. Cook and stir over low heat until very thick and creamy, about 3 minutes. Remove from heat and stir in vanilla, whisky, and rum.

Ladle hot pudding into individual serving dishes. Cover with plastic wrap or waxed paper and refrigerate until cold, about 3 hours. Can be prepared 2 days in advance. Keep refrigerated until ready to serve.

Amaretto Chocolate Pudding
with Amaretto Whipped Cream

An infusion of delectable amaretto and a small amount
of the finest chocolate transform packaged pudding mix into
something quite extraordinary. As an added treat, serve the pudding
in chocolate cups (available at gourmet grocery stores).

SERVES 8

Place pudding mix, chocolate, and milk in a medium saucepan. Over medium heat, stir until chocolate melts and pudding comes to a boil and thickens. (If the mixture looks lumpy, smooth out by whisking.) Remove from heat and let cool 5 minutes. Stir in amaretto. Cover with plastic wrap, pressing the wrap onto the surface of the pudding to prevent a skin from forming. Chill until set. Spoon into serving dishes. Top with Amaretto Whipped Cream (see directions on following page).

1 5-ounce box (cook and serve) chocolate pudding mix

2 ounces good-quality bittersweet or semisweet chocolate, finely chopped

3 cups whole milk or half-and-half (or a combination of both)

¼ cup amaretto liqueur

Amaretto Whipped Cream

1 cup (8 ounces) chilled whipping cream

1 tablespoon sugar

1 tablespoon amaretto

Fresh raspberries and chocolate curls for garnish

Using a chilled bowl and beaters, beat cream on medium-high speed until thick, about 2 minutes. Add sugar and amaretto, beating 2 minutes more or until soft peaks form. Spoon whipped cream atop pudding, or transfer to pastry bag fitted with large star tip and pipe on to pudding. Garnish with raspberries and chocolate curls.

Chocolate needs to be slightly softened in order to make curls. Soften by warming in the microwave for about 30 seconds. Warm white chocolate for 10-15 seconds. (Time will vary depending on the amount and type of chocolate.) Pull a vegetable peeler along side of chocolate, allowing curls to fall gently.

—————————

P I E S

C O O K I E S

a n d

B A R S

—————————

Raspberry Chiffon Cheesecake Pie

Bright ribbons of raspberry puree swirled through creamy white cheesecake adds a nice touch to this simple, no-bake, scrumptious dessert.

SERVES 8

Place mixer bowl and beaters in freezer for about 10 minutes.

Remove bowl and beaters from freezer. Beat cream on medium-high speed until soft peaks form, about 4 minutes. Transfer cream to another bowl and set aside. Using the same mixing bowl (you don't have to wash it out), beat cream cheese at medium speed until creamy. Add lemon juice and ½ cup sugar. Beat until smooth. Beat in whipped cream until mixed well.

In a small saucepan, sprinkle gelatin over ¼ cup cold water. Allow to soften for 1 minute (it will look spongy). Heat mixture over low heat, stirring until gelatin is dissolved and no longer lumpy. Remove from heat. With the mixer running, slowly add half of the gelatin to the cream cheese mixture until fully incorporated. Set remaining gelatin aside.

Process raspberries and remaining 2 tablespoons sugar in food processor until smooth. Force puree through a fine sieve into a bowl, discarding the seeds. Stir Chambord and remaining gelatin into the raspberry mixture.

Drop large spoonfuls of cheesecake batter into the prepared crust, leaving gaps for the raspberry puree. Fill gaps with raspberry puree. Carefully, without breaking the crust, swirl the two mixtures together using a chopstick or the handle of a small wooden spoon. Place in refrigerator for 4 hours. For an elegant look, garnish with fresh raspberries on top of piped whipped cream if desired.

1¼ cups whipping cream

1 pound cream cheese

¼ cup lemon juice

½ cup plus 2 tablespoons sugar (I prefer superfine white granulated sugar because it dissolves nicely)

2 tablespoons gelatin

¼ cup cold water

12 ounces frozen raspberries, slightly thawed

3 tablespoons Chambord or other raspberry liqueur

1 9-inch ready-to-use graham cracker crust

Fresh raspberries and whipped cream for garnish (optional)

Brandy Alexander Pie

Brandy Alexander Pie can easily become Grasshopper Pie
by substituting crème de menthe for the brandy.

SERVES 8

1¼ cups chilled whipping
cream, divided

¼ cup white chocolate liqueur

1¼ teaspoons unflavored
gelatin

9 ounces white chocolate,
chopped

¼ cup brandy

½ cup sour cream

1 chocolate cookie pie crust

White and dark chocolate
curls for garnish
(see sidebar on page 72)

Combine ¼ cup cream and white chocolate liqueur in a medium saucepan. Sprinkle with gelatin and whisk to blend. Let stand 10 minutes to soften. Place saucepan over low heat and stir until gelatin dissolves. Add white chocolate and stir until melted and smooth. Stir in brandy. Transfer mixture to a large bowl and cool, stirring occasionally.

Beat remaining 1 cup cream and sour cream on medium-high speed in a medium bowl until stiff peaks form. Fold cream into white chocolate mixture until well combined. Transfer filling to pie crust. Chill for at least 4 hours.

Place curls decoratively atop cake, mounding slightly, and serve.

To make a double chocolate crust, spread about 3 tablespoons melted chocolate over the crust before adding the pie filling.

Jack Daniel's Chocolate Pecan Pie

Another winner from the nice folks at Jack Daniel's.
This one is so easy, a beginner can easily master it.

SERVES 8

Preheat oven to 375°F. Combine eggs, sugar, butter, corn syrup, vanilla, and Jack Daniel's in a mixing bowl. Blend well. Sprinkle chocolate chips and pecans over bottom of pie shell. Pour in filling. Bake for 35 to 40 minutes or until set. Cool before serving.

3 large eggs, beaten

1 cup granulated sugar

2 tablespoons butter, melted

1 cup corn syrup

1 teaspoon pure vanilla extract

¼ cup Jack Daniel's Tennessee Whiskey

½ cup semisweet chocolate chips

1 cup pecan halves

1 unbaked 10-inch pie shell

Armagnac Pumpkin Pie
with Streusel Topping

This rich, smooth version of pumpkin pie is a Puente family favorite.
For simplicity, I use a store-bought deep-dish pie crust.

SERVES 8

2 eggs, separated

2 tablespoons Armagnac or
brandy

1 15-ounce can pumpkin
puree

1 teaspoon ground cinnamon

½ teaspoon ground ginger

½ teaspoon ground nutmeg

½ teaspoon salt

1 14-ounce can sweetened
condensed milk

1 unbaked 9-inch deep-dish
pie crust

Preheat oven to 425°F. Using an electric mixer on medium-high speed, beat egg whites until fluffy. Transfer to a bowl and set aside.

In the same mixing bowl (it's okay if there's still a bit of egg white in the bowl) on medium speed, blend egg yolks, Armagnac, pumpkin puree, cinnamon, ginger, nutmeg, and salt. Pour in sweetened condensed milk and continue blending until smooth. Gently fold in the egg whites. Pour filling into crust.

Bake 15 minutes. Remove pie from oven. Reduce heat to 325°F and prepare Streusel Topping (see directions on opposite page).

Streusel Topping

Combine flour, brown sugar, and cinnamon. Cut in butter using a pastry blender or by crisscrossing two knives until mixture is crumbly. Mix in walnuts. Sprinkle topping over cooked pumpkin pie. Return pie to oven, and bake at 325°F for an additional 40 minutes or until set.

2 *tablespoons all-purpose flour*

3 *tablespoons packed dark brown sugar*

1 *teaspoon ground cinnamon*

2 *tablespoons butter, chilled*

¾ *cup chopped walnuts*

L'Orange Madeleines
with L'Orange Syrup

These plump, moist, and delightfully tasty teacake-style cookies
will keep for several days in an airtight container.

2 cups cake flour

1 teaspoon baking powder

½ teaspoon salt

4 tablespoons freshly grated
orange zest (colored peel
only, no white pith)

2 sticks (1 cup) unsalted
butter, softened

2 teaspoons fresh orange juice

2 cups sugar

6 large eggs

Preheat oven to 325°F. Lightly coat madeleine molds with a mixture of approximately 1 tablespoon melted butter and 2 teaspoons flour.

In a bowl, whisk together cake flour, baking powder, salt, and zest. In the bowl of an electric mixer, beat together butter, orange juice, and sugar on medium-high speed until mixture is fluffy, about 4 minutes. Add eggs, one at a time, beating well after each addition. Reduce speed to low and add flour mixture, beating until just combined. Spoon batter into prepared madeleine molds until ¾ full.

Bake 15 minutes or until edges are browned and tops are golden. Remove from oven and invert onto a rack set over a cookie sheet. Brush warm madeleines with hot L'Orange Syrup (see directions on page 82). Serve warm or at room temperature.

L'Orange Syrup

¼ cup water

¼ cup sugar

¼ cup Grey Goose Vodka
   L'Orange

¼ cup fresh orange juice

In a small saucepan over medium heat, bring all ingredients to a boil, stirring frequently. While continuing to stir, boil syrup for 8 minutes or until reduced by about half. Remove from heat.

Biscotti

*A visit to the lovely seaside town of Ventura, California, isn't complete without a stop at
Atelier de Chocolat, a quaint little candy shop on Main Street.
Since I'm a loyal customer and fan of all their goodies, they were kind enough to
share their biscotti recipe with me for this book.*

YIELDS 2 DOZEN

Heat oven to 325°F. Using an electric mixer on medium-high speed, cream butter, sugar, and orange zest until fluffy, about 5 minutes. Add eggs, one at a time, beating after each addition. Stir in vanilla. Add amaretto.

Combine dry ingredients; add to butter mixture. Add toasted almonds. Blend well, but don't overmix.

Divide dough into two equal parts. On a greased cookie sheet, pat each piece of dough into a rectangle, about 12 x 5½ inches. Bake 20 minutes or until dough is set but not browned. Remove from oven. While still warm, cut dough into ¾-inch-wide strips. Tip each onto its side and return to oven. Bake until golden brown, about 35 minutes, turning over halfway through baking time for equal browning. Transfer biscotti to racks and cool completely. You can store biscotti in an airtight container at room temperature for up to 2 weeks.

Because biscotti are dry by nature, they are often served with coffee or liqueur, the intention being that they are dipped and eaten.

¾ cup (1½ sticks) unsalted butter, at room temperature

1 cup granulated sugar

1 tablespoon finely grated orange zest (colored peel only, no white pith)

4 eggs

1 teaspoon pure vanilla extract

2 tablespoons amaretto

4½ cups all-purpose flour

4½ teaspoons baking powder

½ teaspoon salt

½ teaspoon cinnamon

¼ teaspoon ground cloves

¼ teaspoon ground coriander

¼ teaspoon ground nutmeg

1½ cups chopped or slivered almonds, toasted (see sidebar on page 87)

Lemon-Lime Margarita Bars with Sugar-Cookie Crust

*Spiked with the flavor of a margarita cocktail, what could be
a more appropriate or delectable way to conclude a spicy Southwestern meal?*

YIELDS 1 DOZEN

CRUST

1 cup unsalted butter,
   at room temperature

2 cups all-purpose flour

½ cup granulated sugar

FILLING

4 large eggs

1½ cups granulated sugar

¼ cup all-purpose flour

Juice of 2 fresh lemons

Juice of 2 fresh limes

Zest of 2 limes (colored peel
   only, no white pith)

¼ cup tequila

Preheat oven to 350°F. Combine butter, flour, and sugar in a large bowl. Firmly press into the bottom of a 13 x 9 x 2-inch pan. Bake about 15 minutes or until light golden. Allow to cool slightly before adding filling.

Whisk together eggs, sugar, flour, fruit juices, zest, and tequila. Pour over baked and slightly cooled cookie crust. Bake an additional 18 minutes or until set. Let cool before slicing.

CHOCOLATE

DESSERTS

Dark Truffle Tart with Walnut Crust

*Try agave nectar instead of corn syrup in this simple, elegant, and tasty dessert.
Available at natural food stores, agave nectar is produced from the core of the blue agave
plant and can be used to sweeten everything from beverages to baked goods.
Because it's much sweeter than sugar, a small amount yields the same sweetness.*

SERVES 10

Place toasted walnuts, agave nectar or corn syrup, and melted butter in food processor. Pulse until mixture is moist and sticky, about 20 seconds. Transfer mixture to an 8- or 9-inch tart pan. (You can also use a spring form pan.) Pat mixture evenly on bottom and sides of pan. Set in freezer while preparing filling.

In a small saucepan over medium heat, bring cream to a simmer. Add chocolate. Remove pan from heat. Stir until smooth. Stir in orange liqueur. Pour chocolate mixture into chilled crust. Refrigerate until set or overnight.

Serve with freshly whipped cream or Classic Crème Fraîche (page 136).

CRUST

2 cups walnuts, toasted

2 tablespoons agave nectar or corn syrup

½ cup (1 stick) unsalted butter, melted

FILLING

1 cup heavy whipping cream

8 ounces dark chocolate, chopped into small pieces

3 tablespoons Cointreau or other orange liqueur

TOASTING TIP

Toasting the nuts will add a wonderful flavor. Simply heat a large nonstick skillet over high heat until very hot. Reduce heat to low. Add nuts and cook, stirring quickly until lightly toasted, 1 to 2 minutes. Do not burn. Or, spread nuts on a baking sheet and bake at 350°F for about 10 minutes.

Sambuca-Espresso Truffle Kisses

*Sambuca, an anise-flavored liqueur often served with coffee beans,
is great with chocolate, especially in these simple goodies.*

YIELDS ABOUT 4 DOZEN

12 ounces fine-quality
bittersweet or dark
chocolate, chopped

½ stick (¼ cup) unsalted
butter, cut into pieces

¼ cup heavy whipping cream

1 tablespoon instant espresso
powder dissolved in 1
tablespoon boiling water

2 tablespoons plus 1 teaspoon
Sambuca or other anise
liqueur

In a large glass or other microwave-safe bowl, place chocolate, butter, cream, and dissolved espresso. Warm on the defrost setting for approximately 6 minutes. Remove and stir until the mixture is smooth and creamy. Stir in liqueur. Cool for about 10 minutes.

Transfer truffle mixture to a pastry bag fitted with a ½-inch plain tip. Pipe mixture onto baking sheet lined with waxed paper, forming little cone-shaped kisses. Twist your wrist when finishing each truffle to create a point.

Chill until firm, at least 2 hours.

Crème de Menthe Truffles

Inspired by the creamy mint-chocolate after-dinner drink, these truffles take just minutes to assemble and can be stored in the refrigerator until ready to serve.

SERVES 4

In a large bowl, mix together vanilla wafers, powdered sugar, pecans, crème de menthe, and agave nectar or corn syrup. Refrigerate for at least 1 hour.

Scoop out mixture with a melon baller. Roll balls in grated chocolate. Keep refrigerated until ready to serve.

1 cup crushed vanilla wafers

1 cup powdered sugar

½ cup finely chopped pecans

⅓ cup crème de menthe

2 tablespoons agave nectar or corn syrup

½ cup grated dark chocolate

Jägermeister Fudgy Brownies
with Jägermeister Chocolate Glaze

If you like Jägermeister herbal liqueur, then you'll love these very chewy brownies.
They'll keep for five days, so they're a great make-ahead dessert. The taste
actually improves with time, so plan on baking the brownies a day or two in advance.

YIELDS ABOUT 1 DOZEN

1 cup flour

⅛ teaspoon salt

½ teaspoon baking powder

2 ounces unsweetened chocolate, chopped into small pieces

4 ounces dark chocolate, chopped into small pieces

10 tablespoons (1¼ sticks) unsalted butter

3 large eggs

1¼ cups sugar

2 teaspoons pure vanilla extract

½ cup Jägermeister

1 cup walnuts, toasted (optional) (see sidebar on page 86)

Preheat oven to 325°F. Butter a 13 x 9 x 2-inch metal baking pan. Dust with cocoa powder, knocking out excess. Or simply line the pan with parchment paper. Whisk flour, salt, and baking powder; set aside. Melt unsweetened and dark chocolate with butter in a double boiler, stirring until smooth. Or, if you prefer (I do!), melt chocolate and butter in microwave for 5 minutes.

Remove chocolate from heat and whisk in eggs, one at a time. Fully incorporate each egg before adding the next. Whisk in sugar, vanilla, and Jägermeister. Continue whisking until mixture is completely smooth. Add dry ingredients to chocolate mixture. Don't overmix. Add nuts. Pour batter into prepared pan and bake in middle of oven until top is firm, about 40 minutes. Cool completely in pan on a rack before cutting into squares. Prepare Chocolate Glaze (see directions on opposite page).

The smaller and deeper the baking pan, the more moist and chewy the brownies will be. Always check brownies 10 minutes before the suggested baking time. If toothpick inserted in the middle comes up with really fudgy crumbs, it's time to take the brownies out and put them on a wire rack for cooling. Fresh-baked brownies will appear slightly undercooked.

Jägermeister Chocolate Glaze

In a medium saucepan over medium heat, bring cream and corn syrup to a simmer. Remove pan from heat. Add chocolate and Jägermeister, whisking until smooth. Pour glaze over cooled brownies.

½ cup whipping cream

2 tablespoons dark corn syrup

9 ounces dark chocolate, finely chopped

2 tablespoons Jägermeister

Cherry Marzipan Balls

*This was the first dessert I made as a little girl. My sisters and I were allowed
to make Cherry Marzipan Balls because they required no baking,
were easy to prepare, and kept us occupied and out of Mom's hair for a while.
Today, the only difference is that we use cherry liqueur instead
of the liquid from Maraschino cherries.*

YIELDS ABOUT 4 DOZEN

1 7-ounce roll marzipan or
almond paste

¼ cup shredded sweetened
coconut

2 tablespoons cherry brandy

GLAZE

3 ounces bittersweet
chocolate

1 tablespoon cherry brandy

Arrange fifty mini–paper cups on a sheet pan. Using an electric mixer fitted with a dough hook attachment, combine marzipan, coconut, and cherry brandy on low speed until soft and well blended. You may also knead by hand until blended. Shape into bite-sized balls. Prepare glaze.

Place chocolate and cherry brandy in a microwave-safe bowl. Melt on the defrost setting for about 3 minutes. Remove and stir until smooth. Dip each ball in melted chocolate and place in a mini–paper cup. Keep cool until ready to serve.

FRUIT

DESSERTS

Bärenjäger Berry Baskets

This light dessert is a great choice for a bridal shower or ladies' luncheon.

SERVES 4

Preheat oven to 350°F. Toss berries with Bärenjäger and set aside. Lightly grease four 1-cup ramekins.

Work with one sheet of phyllo dough at a time, keeping the remaining sheets covered with a damp towel to prevent them from drying out. Cut one sheet into four 6-inch squares. Place a phyllo square on a work surface and brush with melted butter. Butter a second square and lay it on top of the first square at an angle. Take the two remaining phyllo squares and place them one at a time on top of the first two squares, each at a different angle (you will have eight starlike tips). Gently press the stacked squares into a ramekin to form a basket. Repeat with the remaining phyllo dough sheets. Place filled ramekins on a baking sheet. Bake 10 minutes or until golden and crispy. Carefully lift baskets out of ramekins, twisting slightly to loosen; place on rack. Cool completely. (Can be made up to 2 days in advance. Store in airtight container at room temperature.)

Using a chilled bowl and beaters, beat cream on medium-high speed until thickened, about 2 minutes. Add sugar and vanilla, beating 2 minutes longer or until soft peaks form. Fill each basket with cream mixture, either spooned or piped in. Arrange berries on top.

1½ cups assorted red berries

3 tablespoons Bärenjäger honey liqueur

4 sheets phyllo dough, thawed if frozen

2 tablespoons unsalted butter, melted

1 cup heavy whipping cream

1 tablespoon granulated sugar

1 teaspoon pure vanilla extract

Motlow's Butter-Pecan Peach Cobbler

A Lynchburg, Tennessee, favorite flavored with a little of the hometown product.
This recipe is served at Miss Mary Bobo's Boarding House and was
the favorite of the bank president, Tom Motlow, one of Jack Daniel's many relatives.

SERVES 6

FILLING

¾ *cup packed dark brown sugar*

⅓ *cup Jack Daniel's Tennessee Whiskey*

4 *tablespoons butter*

2 *tablespoons all-purpose flour*

10 *cups peeled and sliced fresh peaches*

DUMPLINGS

1½ *cups all-purpose flour*

¼ *cup sugar*

4 *teaspoons baking powder*

1 *teaspoon salt*

½ *cup milk*

3 *tablespoons butter, melted*

½ *teaspoon vanilla*

½ *cup chopped pecans*

Preheat oven to 425°F. In a 12-inch cast-iron skillet or other ovenproof pan, combine brown sugar, Jack Daniel's, butter, and flour. Mix well. Bring to a boil and cook about 2 minutes. Stir in peaches; reduce heat and simmer while preparing dumplings.

In a medium bowl, combine flour, sugar, baking powder, and salt; stir to blend. Add milk, butter, vanilla, and pecans; stir just until dry ingredients are moistened.

Drop batter by tablespoon over peaches simmering in skillet. Remove from stove and place in the heated oven. Bake about 15 minutes or until dumplings are lightly browned. Serve warm with ice cream or whipped cream, or drizzle with heavy whipping cream.

Bananas in Grey Goose L'Orange Caramel

I've adapted this recipe from one by Pascal Courtin, personal chef to businessman Sidney Frank. Chef Courtin flambés the bananas just before serving. This dramatic method of food presentation can be done simply by sprinkling the warm dessert with a small amount of slightly heated liqueur or vodka and igniting it with a match just before serving.

SERVES 6

Combine brown sugar, cream, and butter in an 8-inch frying pan. Stir over low heat until sugar dissolves, about 5 minutes. Increase heat until mixture comes to a boil. Reduce heat and simmer, stirring, for 4 or 5 minutes, or until reduced to a thick caramel glaze. Stir in orange juice and cinnamon. Add bananas and pecans (if using), stirring gently until coated and bananas are slightly cooked but not soggy. Remove from heat. Add vodka and stir.

If you choose to flambé, use a long match, and be careful if you're wearing loose sleeves! When the flames die down, stir to mix flavors. Serve over ice cream.

1 cup packed dark brown sugar

1 cup whipping cream

12 tablespoons (1½ sticks) unsalted butter

Juice from 1 orange

½ teaspoon ground cinnamon

6 medium-sized bananas, cut into 4 pieces (lengthwise and then in half)

½ cup chopped pecans (optional)

½ cup Grey Goose Vodka L'Orange, slightly warmed

Premium vanilla ice cream

Honey and Cinnamon Poached Pears

*I took a classic poached pear in red wine recipe and added
Bärenjäger honey liqueur and cinnamon schnapps to create this lovely and
delicious dessert. The pears taste better if they are cooked
a few days ahead and are turned several times to soak up the sauce evenly.
For this recipe, I prefer using Honig Cabernet Sauvignon.*

SERVES 8

2 cups red wine

½ cup granulated sugar

½ cup Bärenjäger honey
liqueur

½ cup cinnamon schnapps

2 cups water

8 firm Bosc or Bartlett pears

Whipped cream, sour
cream, or Classic Crème
Fraîche (optional)

In a large pot, combine wine, sugar, Bärenjäger, schnapps, and water. Bring to a boil.

Meanwhile, peel pears. Carefully place pears in boiling pot. Reduce heat; gently poach 15 minutes or until pears are close to tender when pricked with a fork.

Remove pears from pot; arrange in a heatproof bowl. Remove liquid from pot and strain back into pot. Simmer until sauce is thick and syrupy, about 20 minutes. Pour over pears. Let cool and serve, or refrigerate up to 1 week before serving, turning pears occasionally. If desired, top with a dollop of whipped cream, sour cream, or Classic Crème Fraîche (page 136) before serving.

FROZEN

DESSERTS

Oranges L'Orange

Serve this tangy and uncomplicated dessert at a summer barbeque.

SERVES 6

Cut a 1-inch slice from the stem end of each orange. Scoop pulp into a large bowl. Discard membrane and seeds. Set orange shells aside.

Add vodka and sorbet to orange pulp, stirring until well mixed. (For a frothier texture, process in a blender until smooth.) Spoon into orange shells. Place filled shells in muffin tins. Freeze until firm, at least 1 hour. Remove from freezer 10 minutes before serving.

6 medium navel oranges

¼ cup Grey Goose Vodka L'Orange or other orange liqueur

2 cups (½ quart) orange sorbet

Cherry Chocolate-Chip Baked Alaska

*Baked Alaska always makes an impressive dinner-party dessert.
Even though everyone knows it's the layer of meringue that prevents the ice cream
from melting, just the idea of ice cream from the oven is still unusual enough
to prompt a few* oohs *and* aahs. *Here's the trick to making it foolproof:
The butane kitchen torch you use to caramelize crème brûlée is perfect for
browning the meringue to perfection every time.*

SERVES 8 TO 10

*1 quart cherry chocolate chip
   ice cream*

*1 12-ounce store-bought
   sponge cake or pound cake*

½ cup cherry liqueur

5 egg whites

½ cup sugar

Line a 1-quart bowl (about 7 inches in diameter) with wax paper, extending it above the rim of the bowl. Pack all of the ice cream into bowl and freeze until very firm.

Cut cake into ¼- to ½-inch slices. Line bottom of an 8-inch springform pan with cake slices, arranging slices as tightly as possible. Brush or drizzle cherry liqueur over cake. Invert frozen ice cream onto cake. Remove bowl, leaving wax paper intact. Place ice cream-topped cake in freezer.

Before serving, prepare meringue. Preheat oven to 500°F. In the bowl of an electric mixer, beat egg whites on medium speed until soft peaks form. Gradually add sugar, beating until stiff peaks form.

Remove springform pan from freezer and place on baking sheet. Remove wax paper and springform ring. Spread meringue over top and sides of frozen cake. Bake 4 minutes or until golden, or use a butane torch. Serve immediately.

If desired, you can freeze the cake for up to 1 week after spreading on the meringue. Remove from freezer and bake just before serving.

Chocolate-Covered Raisin-Rum Ice Cream

For a classic rum raisin ice cream,
the raisins are soaked in rum until plump.
In my version, the ice cream base is flavored with rum
and the raisins are chocolate covered.
This is as good, if not better, than any expensive,
premium ice cream on the market.

SERVES 6

In a medium saucepan, combine cream and milk. Bring to a boil over medium-high heat, stirring frequently. Reduce heat to very low. Whisk together brown sugar and egg yolks until well combined. Ladle out one-third of hot cream mixture and whisk into yolk mixture to temper. Then whisk yolk-and-cream mixture into remaining cream mixture in saucepan. Increase heat to medium-low. Cook custard, whisking constantly, until thickened, about 6 minutes. (Do not boil.)

Pour custard through a fine strainer into a bowl. Let cool to room temperature. Stir in vanilla and rum. Cover bowl and refrigerate until cool.

Transfer custard to an ice cream maker and freeze according to the manufacturer's instructions. Gently stir in chocolate-covered raisins and nuts at the end of the freezing cycle. Serve soft, or transfer to an airtight container and put in freezer to harden.

2 cups heavy whipping cream

1½ cups whole milk

⅔ cup packed brown sugar

6 large egg yolks

1 teaspoon pure vanilla extract

⅓ cup dark rum

1 cup chocolate-covered raisins

½ cup chopped pecans, walnuts, or almonds, or chocolate-covered nuts (optional)

Rose Quartz Sorbet/Granita

I once served this pale pink granita at an intimate dinner party. At the time, I didn't have a name for this appetizing dessert. My dinner guests tried in vain to come up with a proper title. One particular guest with a charming British accent proclaimed, "It looks like rose quartz, and I think I'd be having this in a cabana." The accent happened to belong to actor extraordinaire Tim Curry. The fruity flavor has a hint of guava that blends nicely with the coconut derived from the liqueur. Sweet anticipation.

SERVES 4

4 cups any favorite guava-blended juice drink

1 cup Malibu rum, or any coconut-flavored rum

Fresh berries for garnish

In a large bowl or pitcher, mix the guava drink with the rum. To make a sorbet, pour the mixture into an ice cream maker and freeze according to the manufacturer's instructions. For a granita, pour mixture into a baking dish that will evenly distribute the liquid to a depth of approximately a half-inch. (I like using a 13 x 9 x 2-inch metal pan.) To serve, drag a fork over the surface of the granita to create ice crystals.

Spoon mixture into bowls or martini glasses and garnish with fresh berries. For a more festive look, scoop into the hollowed-out shells of mini-pineapples.

Screaming Hawaiian Sorbet/Granita

2 cups Midori melon liqueur

1 cup Malibu rum or any
coconut-flavored rum

½ cup Grey Goose vodka

½ cup pineapple juice

½ cup water

Fresh berries for garnish

Prepare as on page 106 substituting the ingredients. Spoon mixture into martini glasses and garnish with fresh berries.

Plum and Raspberry Sorbet/Granita

2 cups Gekkeikan plum wine

¼ cup Gekkeikan sake

1 cup Chambord or other
raspberry liqueur

¼ cup fresh lime juice

Fresh mint sprigs for
garnish

Prepare as on page 106 substituting the ingredients. Spoon into chilled wine glasses. Decorate each glass with mint sprigs and serve.

Lemon-Drop Sorbet/Granita

This is a smooth and invigorating refreshement.
For added flavor, top with Raspberry Coulis (page 130).

SERVES 4

Combine sugar, water, and lemon juice in a small saucepan. Simmer, stirring, until sugar dissolves. Remove from heat; set aside to cool. Stir in vodka.

For sorbet, freeze the mixture in an ice cream maker according to the manufacturer's instructions. For granita, pour mixture into a baking dish that will evenly distribute the liquid to a depth of approximately a half-inch. (I like using a 13 x 9 x 2-inch metal pan.) To serve, drag a fork over the surface of the granita to create ice crystals.

Spoon mixture into martini glasses and garnish with fresh berries.

1 cup granulated sugar

1 cup water

1¼ cups fresh-squeezed lemon juice

½ cup Grey Goose vodka

Fresh raspberries for garnish

Coffee Sorbet/Granita

This dessert is a delightful conclusion to a hearty Italian meal.
For best results, use Tia Maria coffee liqueur or Kahlua.

SERVES 6

1 cup water

¼ cup granulated sugar

½ cup espresso or very strong
freshly brewed coffee,
cooled

½ cup Tia Maria or other
coffee liqueur

1 cup cold water

1 teaspoon vanilla

In a small saucepan over medium-high heat, bring water and sugar to a simmer. Stir until sugar is dissolved, about 5 minutes. Remove from heat and pour into medium-sized bowl. When mixture has cooled, mix in espresso, coffee liqueur, cold water, and vanilla. Blend thoroughly.

For sorbet, freeze the mixture in an ice cream maker according to the manufacturer's instructions. For granita, pour mixture into a baking dish that will evenly distribute the liquid to a depth of approximately a half-inch. (I like using a 13 x 9 x 2-inch metal pan.) To serve, drag a fork over the surface of the granita to create ice crystals.

Spoon into chilled stemmed glasses or bowls and serve.

SPECIALTY

DESSERTS

Croquembouche with Orange Caramel

Although this elaborate French dessert has been scaled down and simplified (thank goodness for ready-made cream puffs!), the spun sugar adds an impressive touch. Your friends and family will love it.

SERVES 8

Remove cream puffs from freezer and allow to thaw slightly.

Combine sugar, corn syrup, and water in a heavy medium-sized saucepan. Stir over medium heat until sugar is dissolved, frequently brushing down sides of pan with a wet pastry brush if crystals develop. (See sidebar on caramel on page 67.) Increase heat; boil without stirring, continuing to brush down any crystals until syrup is amber colored, about 10 minutes. Remove from heat and allow to cool about 1 minute. Stir in orange liqueur.

Using tongs, dip each puff into the hot caramel syrup and arrange on a serving platter, stacking puffs into a pyramid shape.

When done, dip tongs into the caramel and place a drop of caramel at the bottom of the pyramid. With the end of the tongs, gently pull the caramel syrup, spinning it into threads. Continue spinning and whirling strands of caramel around the puffs, forming a spun-sugar web that encases the entire pyramid.

Serve within a few hours.

1 17.6 ounce (34 puffs) box frozen mini–cream puffs

2 cups sugar

1 tablespoon corn syrup

1 cup water

¼ cup orange liqueur

Black Forest Trifle

*I developed this recipe with a little help from my sister Judi. I took elements from both
a Black Forest cake and a trifle to create this delicious all-in-one dessert.
I use a store-bought cake for convenience. The bakery department of your local grocery store
will often sell cake layers without frosting at a reasonable price.*

SERVES 12

Chocolate Cherry Mousse
(page 60)

1 14- to 16-ounce prepared
chocolate cake

½ cup cherry brandy

3 cups pitted fresh or
frozen cherries, halved

TOPPING

1 cup heavy whipping cream

¼ cup powdered sugar

Whole cherries with stems

¼ cup sliced almonds, toasted
(see sidebar on page 86)

Chocolate curls
(see sidebar on page 72)

Prepare Chocolate Cherry Mousse. Refrigerate until needed. (Can be
made 1 or 2 days ahead.)

Cut cake into thin slices. Line bottom of trifle bowl (or other decorative
glass serving bowl) with a third of the cake slices. Sprinkle with a third of
the cherry brandy. Spoon a third of the cherries over cake. Top with a
third of the mousse. Repeat the layering process, ending with mousse on
top. Cover and refrigerate until well chilled, or up to a day ahead. Before
serving, prepare topping.

Beat cream and powdered sugar on medium-high speed until stiff peaks
form. Transfer to a pastry bag fitted with a star tip. Pipe cream down center of trifle. Pipe rosettes around edge. Top rosettes with whole cherries.
Sprinkle trifle with almonds and chocolate curls. Keep refrigerated until
ready to serve.

Chocolate Raspberry Tiramisu

I really like make-ahead desserts.
This is my interpretation of the classic Italian dessert using Chambord
(my favorite liqueur) and raspberries (my favorite fruit).
If fresh raspberries are out of season, frozen raspberries will work just as well.

SERVES 6

In a large bowl, blend cheese, sugar, 2 tablespoons espresso, 3 table-spoons Chambord, and egg yolks until creamy. Set aside in a cool place. In a clean bowl, whip egg whites on medium speed until firm. Fold into cheese mixture until well combined.

In a bowl, mix remaining espresso with remaining Chambord. Quickly dip about half the ladyfingers in the espresso-Chambord mixture, turning to coat lightly. Arrange on bottom of pretty serving bowl. Cover bottom completely, trimming or breaking ladyfingers to fit.

Spoon half of cheese mixture over ladyfingers; smooth top. Sprinkle with half the raspberries and half the shaved chocolate. Dip more ladyfingers and arrange over chocolate, covering completely and trimming to fit. Gently spread remaining mascarpone mixture over ladyfingers; smooth top. Sprinkle with remaining raspberries and chocolate. Cover; chill at least 4 hours or overnight.

1 pound mascarpone cheese (Italian cream cheese) or regular cream cheese

4 tablespoons sugar

1 cup espresso or very strong brewed coffee, divided

4 tablespoons Chambord or other raspberry liqueur, divided

4 eggs, separated

1 7-ounce package ladyfingers (24 7-inch biscuits)

½ cup raspberries

4 tablespoons shaved or finely grated chocolate

Southern Comfort Caramel Peach Crêpes

There's more to crêpes than Suzette!

SERVES 6

FILLING

6 tablespoons unsalted butter

1 cup Southern Comfort

¼ cup granulated sugar

4 large fresh peaches, pitted, peeled, and sliced

CRÊPES

1⅓ cups milk, at room temperature

1 cup flour

3 eggs

3 tablespoons unsalted butter, melted, plus additional for brushing

1 tablespoon sugar

¼ teaspoon salt

Vegetable oil cooking spray or butter

Place butter, Southern Comfort, and sugar in a medium saucepan. Bring to a boil over medium heat, stirring frequently. Reduce heat to a simmer, cooking until sauce thickens, about 8 minutes. Add peaches to simmering sauce, stirring gently. Continue to simmer, stirring occasionally, until sauce is thick, golden brown, and caramelized, about 10 minutes. Cool the peach mixture to room temperature.

In a blender, combine milk, flour, eggs, butter, sugar, and salt. Blend until just smooth. Cover batter and chill at least 15 minutes or up to 1 day.

Coat a 7-inch-diameter nonstick skillet with vegetable oil spray, or film skillet with butter. Place over medium heat. Pour 2 tablespoons batter into pan and swirl to coat bottom. Cook until edge of crêpe is golden, about 30 seconds. Loosen edges gently with spatula. Carefully turn crêpe over, using your fingers if necessary. (If you've never made crêpes before, it may take several tries before you get the hang of it.) Cook until bottom begins to brown slightly, about 20 seconds. Transfer to plate. Cover with paper towel. Repeat with remaining batter, coating pan with spray as needed and covering each crêpe with a paper towel when done.

Before serving, preheat oven to 350°F. Spoon peach filling into center of crêpes and fold twice (into fourths). Place crêpes in a large baking dish, overlapping them slightly. Brush crêpes lightly with melted butter. Cover dish with foil. Bake, covered, until heated through, about 15 minutes. Serve with a premium vanilla ice cream if desired.

Cajeta Caramel Napoleons

Cajeta is a traditional Latin caramel made from sugar and goat's milk. Armagnac enhances the caramel and further underscores the combination of flavors in this already refined dessert.

SERVES 6

PASTRY LAYERS

1 package (17.3-ounces) frozen puff pastry, thawed

2 tablespoons unsalted butter, melted

Granulated sugar for sprinkling

CARAMEL SAUCE

1½ cups granulated sugar

1 tablespoon light corn syrup

½ cup water

1 cup whipping cream, warmed

1 cup goat's milk, warmed

2 tablespoons unsalted butter

2 tablespoons Armagnac

Powdered sugar for dusting

Preheat oven to 400°F. Roll out one puff pastry sheet on lightly floured surface to make a 13 x 10-inch rectangle, trimming if necessary. Cut in half lengthwise, forming two 13 x 5-inch rectangles. Pierce dough all over with fork. Place on a baking sheet. Repeat with remaining pastry sheet. Brush the tops of all four rectangles with melted butter. Sprinkle each with about 1 teaspoon sugar. Bake 14 to 16 minutes, rotating baking sheet about halfway through baking time for even browning. Remove from oven when pastries are golden brown. Set aside until ready to assemble.

Combine sugar, corn syrup, and water in a large saucepan. Stir over medium heat until sugar is dissolved, frequently brushing down sides of pan with a wet pastry brush. Increase heat; boil without stirring until syrup turns a deep golden caramel color, occasionally brushing down sides and swirling pan, about 10 minutes. Remove from heat. Stir in cream, goat's milk, and butter. When slightly cooled, stir in Armagnac.

Arrange three of the pastry rectangles on a large, clean baking sheet. Drizzle each with 2 tablespoons caramel sauce. Reserve plain pastry rectangle for the top. Align pastry layers directly on top of one another. Press assembled pastry lightly so layers will adhere. Cover; chill at least 8 hours and up to 1 day. Refrigerate remaining caramel sauce.

Using serrated knife, cut pastry into six serving pieces. Dust with powdered sugar. Transfer to plates. Warm remaining caramel sauce over low heat; drizzle sauce decoratively onto each plate.

———————————

NOT SO

ELEGANT

but

EASY AND FUN

DESSERTS

———————————

Fruit Jewels

This collegiate favorite has been given a new life as a sophisticated alternative to typical gelatin shots. The possibilities are endless, given the assortment of fruit and gelatin flavors available today. Have fun creating combinations of your favorite fruits and liqueurs. For example, try lime with tequila; grapefruit, lemon, and orange with vodka; kiwi with sake; or papaya with rum. Or use vodka with any or all of the fruits.

YIELDS 3 OR 4 SERVINGS FOR EACH FRUIT

Cut fruits in half lengthwise. Using a melon baller or grapefruit spoon, scrape out and discard all pulp. Set empty shells on a large baking sheet. (If shells are wobbly, set in muffin cups or small bowls.)

Put gelatin in a large bowl with a pouring spout. Add boiling water and stir until completely dissolved. Stir in liqueur. Pour gelatin into shells until each is half full. (Use a spoon to fill the kumquats.) To prevent spills and for easier handling, place shells in refrigerator and pour remaining gelatin to fill. Cover loosely with plastic wrap and refrigerate at least 2 hours. Can be prepared up to 2 days in advance.

KIWI

6 kiwis

1 box (3 ounces) strawberry-kiwi gelatin or lime gelatin

1 cup boiling water

⅔ cup sake

KUMQUATS

1 pound kumquats (about 40, depending on size)

1 box (3 ounces) orange gelatin

¾ cup boiling water

¾ cup Grey Goose Vodka L'Orange or other orange liqueur

CONTINUED

LEMONS

6 *lemons*

1 *box (3 ounces) lemon gelatin*

1 *cup boiling water*

⅔ *cup lemon-flavored vodka, chilled*

LIMES

6 *limes*

1 *box (3 ounces) lime gelatin*

1 *cup boiling water*

⅔ *cup tequila, chilled*

ORANGES

3 *navel oranges*

1 *box (3 ounces) orange gelatin*

1 *cup boiling water*

⅔ *cup Grey Goose Vodka L'Orange or other fruit-flavored vodka, chilled*

As on page 121, cut fruits in half lengthwise. Using a melon baller or grapefruit spoon, scrape out and discard all pulp. Set empty shells on a large baking sheet. (If shells are wobbly, set in muffin cups or small bowls.)

Put gelatin in a large bowl with a pouring spout. Add boiling water and stir until completely dissolved. Stir in liqueur. Pour gelatin into shells until each is half full. To prevent spills and for easier handling, place shells in refrigerator and pour remaining gelatin to fill. Cover loosely with plastic wrap and refrigerate at least 2 hours. Can be prepared up to 2 days in advance.

S'mores Con Amour

*This recipe was given to me by Regina Charboneau, chef de cuisine
at Monmouth Plantation in Natchez, Mississippi. She adds Tia Maria, a rich, delicious
coffee liqueur, transforming the simple s'more into something quite sophisticated.*

SERVES 4

Tear off four pieces of aluminum foil, each 12 x 8 inches. In a large bowl, toss marshmallows with Tia Maria. Place one graham cracker atop each piece of foil. Top with one piece of chocolate, three marshmallows, pecans (if using), and graham cracker. Fold each piece of foil into an envelope shape to allow for easier unwrapping.

Using long tongs, hold each s'more a few inches above a fireplace or campfire for about 3 minutes. Unwrap and enjoy.

12 large marshmallows

½ cup Tia Maria

8 small graham cracker sheets

2 8-ounce bars bittersweet or dark chocolate, divided into 4 pieces

Sliced pecans (optional)

French-Kissed Watermelon

I first saw this recipe in the September 1989 issue of Gourmet *magazine
as Peach Schnapps and Vodka Plugged Watermelon.
Over the years I've made this on several occasions and found that using
orange-flavored vodka really improves the taste.
When I learned that there is a mixed drink made with Grey Goose Vodka L'Orange and
peach schnapps called French Kiss, the new name suggested itself.
Serve French-Kissed Watermelon on a hot day—your guests will love it.*

SERVES 8

*1 whole watermelon
(approximately 12 pounds)*

*1 to 1½ cups peach schnapps
or peach brandy*

*1 to 1½ cups Grey Goose
Vodka L'Orange*

Stand the watermelon on end in a large bowl (or in your kitchen sink),
stem end up. Cut out a 3-inch-diameter plug around the stem similar to
a jack-o'-lantern lid. Remove the plug and set aside. Scoop out about
4 inches of the flesh, and pour out the excess liquid.

With a long skewer, pierce the flesh inside to the bottom and in all directions without penetrating the rind. Pour out any excess liquid. Gradually
pour equal amounts of peach schnapps and vodka into the watermelon
until it cannot absorb any more. Replace the plug. Chill the watermelon
on end overnight or up to 2 days. You may have to remove a shelf from the
refrigerator to fit the melon. Cut the watermelon into wedges and serve.

Jägermeister Root Beer Float

This is one of the simplest indulgences I know.

Root beer is made from extractions from various roots and herbs. So is Jägermeister.

Together they're perfect, and with ice cream they're even better.

SERVES 2

Fill two tall glasses two-thirds full with equal parts Jägermeister and root beer. Top each with a scoop of ice cream. Serve with straws and long-handled spoons.

1 cup Jägermeister, chilled

16 ounces root beer, chilled

2 scoops vanilla ice cream

SAUCES

a n d

ACCOMPANIMENTS

Cherries Jubilee

It's hard to believe that something so delectable can be so simple. Cherries, brandy, wine, about 10 minutes in the kitchen, and you've created a classic dessert. I experimented with many different red wines and discovered that Honig Cabernet Sauvignon created a savory balance of flavors.

SERVES 4

In a bowl, mix cherry juice, cherry brandy, and wine. In a small saucepan, stir sugar and cornstarch until mixed. Gradually whisk in wine mixture, then cherries. Over medium-high heat, bring sauce to a boil, stirring gently. Continue stirring until sauce thickens, about 5 minutes. Remove from heat. Stir in almond extract.

Divide ice cream among four bowls and spoon warm sauce on top. For a showy presentation, add a little extra cherry brandy to the finished sauce and heat gently without stirring. Ignite and spoon the flaming sauce over ice cream.

1 1-pound bag frozen unsweetened pitted dark sweet cherries, thawed, drained, juice reserved

¼ cup cherry brandy

¼ cup red wine

3 tablespoons sugar

1 tablespoon cornstarch

⅛ teaspoon almond extract

1 quart vanilla or cherry vanilla ice cream

Raspberry Coulis

When berry season rolls around, this tangy sauce adds simple elegance
to fruit platters, sorbets, pound cake, or waffles.

YIELDS ABOUT 1 CUP

2 cups raspberries

1 tablespoon sugar

1 tablespoon lemon juice

2 tablespoons Chambord or
Framboise Royale

Combine all ingredients in a food processor or blender and process until smooth. Strain through a fine-mesh strainer to remove seeds. Cover and refrigerate until needed.

Jack Daniel's Famous Caramel Sauce

For an instant, impressive dessert, always keep a batch of caramel sauce
in the refrigerator to pour over ice cream, fresh or poached fruits, bread pudding, or cake.
The sauce will keep for a few weeks.

YIELDS 2 CUPS

½ cup (1 stick) butter

1 cup dark brown sugar

½ cup heavy whipping cream

¼ cup Jack Daniel's Tennessee
Whiskey

Melt butter in saucepan. Stir in sugar and cream. Bring to a boil over medium heat, stirring constantly. Remove from heat and pour into a bowl to cool. Whisk in Jack Daniel's. Serve warm or at room temperature. Store remainder in refrigerator.

Fluffy Orange Dip for Fruit

You can use any sliced fresh fruit with this delicious dip,
but my favorites are bananas, green apples, and strawberries.

SERVES 4

Whip together all ingredients except fruit until very fluffy. Keep refrigerated until ready to serve. Can be prepared a day in advance. Serve with sliced fruit for dipping.

1 7-ounce jar marshmallow cream

1 8-ounce package cream cheese, softened

Zest of 1 orange (colored peel only, no white pith)

3 tablespoons Cointreau or other orange liqueur

Any favorite fruit

Kumquat Sake Sauce

This bright and wonderfully tangy sauce is great
with ice cream, yogurt, or pound cake.

YIELDS 2 CUPS

In a medium saucepan, bring the water, sake, and sugar to a boil. Reduce heat and simmer for 6 minutes. Stir in the kumquats and increase heat to medium-high. Boil until thickened and glossy, about 7 minutes. Serve the sauce warm or at room temperature.

¼ cup water

¼ cup sake

¼ cup sugar

1 pound kumquats (about 40), trimmed, sliced thin, seeds discarded

Chocolate Armagnac-Spiked Fondue

To create the perfect balance of flavors and texture, use a fine-quality
unsweetened cocoa powder and a mixture of both white and brown sugars.
I also use this recipe as a wonderful sauce to spoon over ice cream
or over Chocolate Melt Cakes (page 33) as a substitute for the L'Orange Sauce.
The sauce can be refrigerated for up to 2 weeks.

SERVES 6

1½ cups heavy whipping cream

9 tablespoons (1 stick plus 1 tablespoon) unsalted butter

1 cup granulated sugar

1 cup tightly packed dark brown sugar

1½ cups fine-quality unsweetened cocoa, sifted

⅛ teaspoon salt

½ cup Saint Vivant Armagnac or other fine brandy

Heat the cream and butter in a medium saucepan over medium heat until just simmering. Add the sugars, stirring until completely dissolved. Remove from heat and cool slightly, about 5 minutes. Add cocoa and salt, whisking until smooth. Whisk in Armagnac. Transfer to fondue pot on warm setting. Serve with suggested accompaniments.

SUGGESTED ACCOMPANIMENTS

Cubed pound cake, fresh strawberries, sliced apples or pears, sliced bananas, fresh tangerine segments, orange slices, sliced star fruit, ladyfingers, or marshmallows.

Passion Sabayon

*Sabayon (also called zabaglione) is a custard sauce that
is whisked over hot water until light and foamy.
It's an appetizing accompaniment to fresh fruit or plain cakes.
The addition of colorful passion fruit seeds adds
a pretty contrast to the pale yellow froth.*

YIELDS ABOUT 2 CUPS

Combine egg yolks and sugar in the upper saucepan of a double boiler. Using a hand-held electric mixer or a large whisk, beat mixture until thick. Set pan over lower saucepan filled with simmering water. While continuing to beat, gradually add Alize. Beat until sabayon mixture is thick and foamy, about 5 minutes. Remove from heat and let cool to room temperature.

Beat cream on medium-high speed to stiff peaks. Whisk in sabayon. Cover and refrigerate until well chilled. (Can be prepared one day ahead.) Before serving, sprinkle with passion fruit seeds if desired.

6 egg yolks

1 tablespoons granulated sugar

1 cup Alize passion fruit liqueur

½ cup heavy whipping cream, well chilled

Passion fruit seeds (optional)

Kiwi-Lime Sauce

For a delightfully refreshing dessert,
dress up melon balls and kiwi slices with a splash of this Midori-based sauce.

YIELDS 1/2 CUP

2 kiwis

1/4 cup Midori melon liqueur

2 tablespoons freshly squeezed
lime juice

Peel and quarter the kiwis. In a food processor or blender, combine kiwis, Midori, and lime juice. Process until smooth. Cover and refrigerate until needed.

Peach Glaze

This glaze is great for sponge cake or pound cake.

YIELDS ABOUT 1 CUP

1 8-ounce jar peach jam
or peach preserves

2 tablespoons peach brandy
or peach schnapps

Combine peach jam and peach brandy in a small saucepan. Warm over low heat until heated through and glossy. Serve warm.

Classic Crème Fraîche

Many of the desserts in this book are enhanced by the addition of crème fraîche,
a sophisticated French cream with a slightly tangy, nutty flavor and velvety rich texture.
Crème fraîche is available in upscale supermarkets, but it's simple and inexpensive
to make at home. It's delicious spooned over fresh fruits, puddings, or cobblers.
Use anywhere from 1 tablespoon to ½ cup buttermilk depending on the tartness you desire.
Also, using more buttermilk will keep the crème fraîche lighter and lower in fat.

YIELDS ABOUT 1 CUP

1 cup heavy whipping cream

2 tablespoons buttermilk,
low-fat or regular

Mix cream and buttermilk in a large bowl. Let stand, covered, at room temperature for 24 hours. If your kitchen is very cold, place the mixture in a gas oven with just the heat from the pilot light. Refrigerate, covered, for another 24 hours to thicken. Will keep 7 to 10 days in the refrigerator, covered (glass jars work very well). Can be whipped if desired before serving.

INDEX

All page numbers in italics refer to photographs

Debbie Puente, author of the 1998 book *Elegantly Easy Crème Brûlée and Other Custard Desserts,* is a recipe consultant and well-known food writer who has written for numerous publications. Debbie can be seen regularly on HGTV's *Smart Solutions*. She resides in Southern California with her husband and three sons.

For questions or comments, please contact the author at liqueurdesserts@hotmail.com.